SET APART

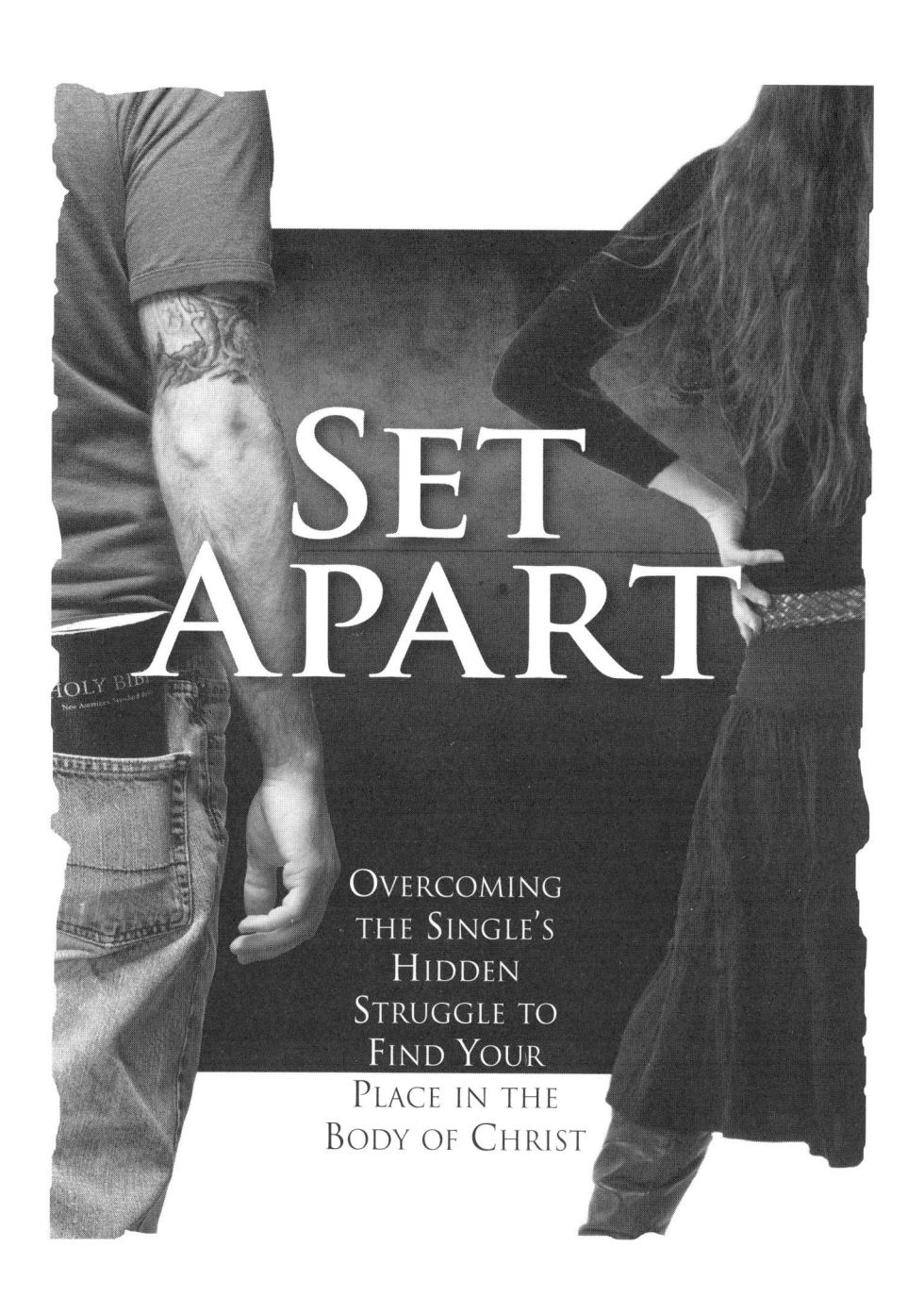

SET APART

OVERCOMING
THE SINGLE'S
HIDDEN
STRUGGLE TO
FIND YOUR
PLACE IN THE
BODY OF CHRIST

AZUKA OKAH

DESTINY IMAGE™ EUROPE srl
Via Maiella, 1
66020 San Giovanni Teatino (Ch) – Italy

"Changing the world, one book at a time."

This book and all other Destiny Image™ Europe books are available at Christian bookstores and distributors worldwide.

To order products, or for any other correspondence:

DESTINY IMAGE™ EUROPE srl
Via Acquacorrente, 6
65123 – Pescara – Italy
Tel. +39 085 4716623 – Fax +39 085 9431270
E:mail: info@eurodestinyimage.com
Or reach us on the Internet: **www.eurodestinyimage.com**

ISBN: 978-88-89127-85-8
For Worldwide Distribution, Printed in U.S.A.
1 2 3 4 5 6 7 8/13 12 11 10 09

ACKNOWLEDGMENTS

I owe immense gratitude to my heavenly Father, the all-knowing God, who gives ability and insight. I offer thanks also to Jesus, my friend and companion, and to the Holy Spirit for His inspiration.

I also owe heartfelt gratitude to Jonathan Atiri, my kindred spirit; my mum, Mrs. Onah; my brother, Dr. Ifeanyi Onah; and William Amangabara. To my husband, Henry, and my children, Eniye, Tari, Ebimi, and Didi: you are God's added blessings in my life. To Destiny Image Europe: thanks for taking this book on board. And to Henry Essang, Youm Adebule, Efiong Isang, and Jean-Jacques Tshowa: you made this book possible.

Finally, to those who enhanced my walk through life and uttered prayers on my behalf, God bless you all.

CONTENTS

FOREWORD

Compressed with information, pregnant with revelation knowledge, this book contains explicit, concise biblical truths to inform and liberate those who are single, married, widowed, and separated. Together let's discover:

- **Our capabilities despite** *the struggle within* **our souls.** With our weaknesses and shortcomings all bared, let's stretch out to the uniqueness that God has given.

- **The gift of being single.** A gift is what it is whether you like it or not. It carries with it certain blessings and the ability to live within its boundaries. You cannot change it; you can only ignore it.

- **The truth about loneliness.** Many people enter marriage because they are lonely, but there will always be seasons of loneliness in the human life. It is a phase of growth that can inspire deep thought and introspection.

- **Reasons for an eagerness to marry.** Nothing can satisfy you except the will of God, not even the marriage partner you seek.

- **Thoughts on touching each other.** This is one area girls love. They may not want the real thing (sex), but they have a desire to be cuddled. Unfortunately, most men don't want to stop at simply holding hands. Touching gives girls a feeling of security, love, warmth, and compassion, but men find it arousing. So hey! No touching!

- **What maturity is not:** Maturity has nothing to do with clothing, talent, educational qualifications, or good job opportunities. Many believers lose their identities because they are trying to be like the crowd. They throw away their natural friendliness for a flimsy façade that doesn't suit them. They become bottled up, change their wardrobes, and shake hands rather than hug one another. They cannot jump and praise God anymore. They cannot cry because of their makeup and are distracted by their jewelry. So…if this is not maturity, what is it?

- **Much more.** This book is long overdue. Come join us as we embark on an adventure of discovery.

The late *Pastor Jonathan Atiri*
Beautiful Gate Assembly
Enugu, Nigeria

Preface

I strongly believe that there is beauty and a lesson to be learned in every pathway we tread in life. Whether we are lonely, crushed, widowed, strong, or weak-willed, God is willing to take His walk with us.

If you have conflicting desires and feel you have lost the desire to reach out and expand, this book is especially for you. I believe those who survive are the *ones* who are *sensitive* to God, who created them, and the Holy Spirit. He obviously has all the answers. Sensitivity to Him who longs to anchor and direct our lives is what we need most. He is the one to *rest* on while we are on life's shore. Sensitivity to Him gives *purpose* to our lives.

What purpose would it serve to run away from our Creator? He is our God. Where would we run anyway? Should we turn to things that *don't really* matter? Running away from Him who gives real meaning to life is a *futile* flight. The Holy Spirit is a person, like our friends, spouses, and parents. He has a distinct personality that can be *felt* in our lives. His power and presence are *evident*. He comes to *energize* as well as *comfort* us. He is the Spirit of God, sent from God.

I pray this book will bring your relationship with God to a *new* peak. I hope you will learn that your mistakes do not need to crush you. God can use them to build you up and draw you closer to Him. May God give you the understanding that can only come from Him, the strength to make the *right decisions*, and the *ability* to live by His good counsel.

I ask our Almighty God to lift your burdens and anxieties, *still* your fears, and stretch out His mighty hand to draw you to Himself. He freely gives His wisdom, and His mercy and grace are sufficient for you.

Introduction

Our contemporary society, customs, and traditions have emphasized that maturity and marriage are synonymous. This is a grievous fallacy because it diffuses the focus of most Christians from giving the best within their capacity no matter their status.

No one informs the unmarried that there can be joy, fulfillment, satisfaction, and pleasure during the long period of their single status.

What about the married? In periods of isolation, they may be burdened with loneliness, pressure, and a desire to fulfill a suppressed calling, wondering if they have waited too long. What of those whose hearts are heavy with beliefs they wish to expound or explore? Those who feel they have waited too long for these to materialize?

I feel a harsh crushing pang in my heart and spirit each time I observe the cruel negligence and lack of revelation given to these experiences. These far outnumber those of the *secure married* walking in their calling. Few books are dedicated to the conflict within the souls of others in their pathetic plight. This book singularly devotes its rich resources to our most secret thoughts and fears, how to make the most intelligent and resourceful use of our singular resolves—if encouraged to step out. *Encouragement* cannot be played down in our ever-*evolving* society.

Most mistakes inspire growth, development, and maturity. However, some have devastating effects and cause scars of deep regret that may be carried for a lifetime. This book of instruction and revelation is prayerfully written to help you avoid those mistakes and decisions that cannot be corrected.

For those of you who think your mistakes are too gross for any kind of amendment or correction, you can change your sorrow into joy by learning that, "Even if we feel guilty, God is *greater* than our feelings and He knows *everything*" (1 John 3:20 NLT). And then we read in Romans 8:28, "We know that all things work together for good to those who love God, to those who are the called according to *His* purpose" (NKJV). God can compensate for your mistakes. He forgives you *and* then forgets what He forgave you for.

Mistakes have nothing to do with age
What you have done is done and gone
It doesn't matter what you have done
Get up, let's dust ourselves and trot on
There is no sin, no woman or man
Whom you love so much
That is valuable enough
To deprive you of heaven

1
THE IN-LOVE SYNDROME

To be in love is not really a constant in our lives, but we can make it so. To be in love involves *intensity* and being *ultra-sensitive* to another person's feelings, mentally and emotionally. This is the height or climax in any relationship. At this stage, a person might even attempt to die for the other. That's how intense these emotions become. They can be overwhelming. Couples who do not just love themselves but are *in love* feel this. Now intensity follows the state of being *in love* all the time. Being in love is not a physical attribute. It *wells* up from the heart. The soul, from the depths of the heart, feels it before the body catches up. The in-love emotion comprised of *bodily desire* is called *eros*.

We'll be looking at desire, yearning, and longing that is synonymous with being in love. When a person is in love with a spouse or loved one, that person desires always to be in the *presence* of the beloved.

The delightful thing I have found out is that God is *in love* with us, the whole of mankind. He has intense feelings for us all the time. He doesn't want us to have cold or lukewarm feelings for Him either! Let's look at this very closely.

The Love of God

For those who desire to love and be loved, it's time we take a journey to the heart of God. First of all, you've got to know that love *binds* the trinity—God the Father, God the Son, and God the Holy Spirit. God the Father loves Jesus and loves the Holy Spirit. Remember what binds them all together? That's right—love. God is love. God loves His Son so much that "all things were made for Him." We read that "All things were made by Him, and nothing was made without Him. In Him there was life, and that life was the light of all people" (John 1:3-4 NCV). This life is what all humans depend on God for, life to live as mortals and life to live eternally as God's children.

"No one can see God, but Jesus Christ [His Son] is exactly like Him. He [Jesus] ranks higher than everything that has been made. Through His power all things were made—things in *heaven* and on *earth*, things *seen* and *unseen*, all powers, authorities, lords, and rulers. All things were made through Christ and for Christ. He was there *before* anything was made, and all things continue *because* of Him" (Col. 1:15-17 NCV).

Doesn't all this *prove* the love God has for His Son? God *is* love! The Holy Spirit is love incarnate. He brings the very fruit of love. He is so tender that you can grieve Him. Even the Father and Jesus are aware of this. Remember, the Spirit is God dwelling in you. This is proof that you *belong* to him. (See Ephesians 4:30.) I believe God the Father and God the Son are protective about the Holy Spirit, so much so that a sin against Him cannot be forgiven. (See Matthew 12:31.) We are warned not to grieve the Holy Spirit or deliberately make Him sad. The Holy Spirit is gentle indeed. Our triune God is protective as they are one and entwined in one another. Jesus said, "I will ask the *Father* [God] and He will give you another helper [the Holy Spirit] to be with you [the person] forever" (John 14:16 NCV).

Finally, listen to this: "But the fruit of the Spirit is love, joy, peace, longsuffering, gentleness, goodness, faith" (Gal. 5:22). This is exactly what I call the *actions of love*! Love *comes* from the Holy Spirit as a first fruit. To us the fruit can equivalently be called love, for "Love is patient and kind. Love is not jealous, it does not brag, and it is not proud. Love is not rude, is not selfish, and does not get upset with others. Love does not count up wrongs that have been done. Love takes no pleasure in evil but rejoices over the truth. Love patiently accepts all things. It always trusts, always hopes, and always endures. Love never ends" (1 Cor. 13:4-8 NCV). Love certainly *is* the answer to all things. It brings joy and peace. It is long-suffering, gentle, and good, and it has faith.

To see how much love and *oneness* are transferred between us (God and mankind), we need only look at the new birth of the believer. As God the Father, the Son, and the Holy Spirit *are* one, *so are we* in them at the new birth. This is a *direct* result of love, the very nature of God. "If people love me, they will obey my teaching. My Father will love them, and we will come to them and make *our home* with them" (John 14:23 NCV). And Jesus said, "On that day you will know that *I am in My Father*, and that *you are in Me* and *I am in you*" (John 14:20 NCV).

This totally consuming love—a love where one person is so lost in the other that neither knows where one begins and the other ends—is God's heart for us. Listen to Jesus again: "I will ask the Father and He will give you another help to be *with you forever*…you know Him because He lives with you and He will be in you." This is the *in-love* syndrome!

Jesus talks to God again: "I have given these people the glory that You gave Me so that *they can be one*, just as *You and I are one*. I will be in them and You will be in Me so that they will be completely one" (John 17:22-23 NCV). We are all *one* and *complete* in one another.

Let us look at how it all started regarding God's love and the giving of *Himself* to us. Then God said, "Let us [God the father,

God the son, God the Holy Spirit] make human beings in Our image and likeness" (Gen. 1:26 NCV). We were created in the image and likeness of our maker; He's the sculptor.

We should note that all things in creation *bear after their kind*. More so us! We are the product of God's type. That's God's law of nature! A banana cannot bring forth yams. So God cannot produce less! God made us "*like Him.*" He therefore deposited His creative abilities in us. He gave us *love,* too, that bit of Himself that is made of intensity, the *In-Love* Syndrome!

It should be noted that Adam didn't tell God that he was lonely or that he needed a helpmate. It was God who saw that. "Then the Lord God said, 'It is not good for man to be alone. I will make him a helper who is right for him'" (Gen. 2:18 NCV).

In-Love *gives*, remember? God made the world for Christ and through Christ. He loved His Son *so* much that "all things were made through Christ and *for* Christ" (Col. 1:16 NCV). Both visible and invisible things! Same for us! He made us lords over all things that He created over the earth. "So God created human beings in His image…. He created them male and female. God blessed them and said, 'Have many children and grow in number. Fill the earth and be *its master*'" (Gen. 1:27-28 NCV). It was the love of God, *His love for us,* that made Him create *Eve* for Adam. He gave Eve to Adam *out* of love. As far as I am concerned, Eve was *a love offering,* along with everything else God created on earth, to Adam, who represents all mankind.

Made in God's Image

Now let us look at the nature of Adam. He was made in the image of God, wasn't he? We should then give back to God that *intensity* that is In-Love; *this is from God Himself!* It is not just a human feeling. *Who* said so? We have just failed to realize that God is in love with us! Who says we shouldn't *pant* after God? David said, "As the deer pants for the water brooks, so pants my soul for You, O God" (Ps. 42:1 NKJV). Why should we not cry in God's presence?

One thing I love and have never seen anywhere else in the Bible is this scripture quotation found in Luke 1:35, which says, "The power of the Highest will overshadow you" (NKJV). The overshadowing of the Virgin Mary caused her to *conceive and bear* a Son! Overshadowing here is like an *entrenchment.* How wonderful! Never have I seen it anywhere else. What is close to this is the *indwelling* of the Holy Spirit in Christians when they *burst* into the *speaking of tongues.* (See Acts 2:4.) The indwelling of the Holy Spirit should produce *fruit* in us, the fruit of the Holy Spirit. This makes us *become* like Him, *one with Him,* literally *new* creations, changed beings!

We should *ache* to be in His presence, to be *overshadowed* by Him, entrenched in Him. The Holy Spirit *aches* to remain in us, to *prune* us so that we *produce* fruit—the fruit of His Spirit—and become *one* with Him. This is how we ought to be as He dwells within us.

Adam could only produce according to his nature. And this nature came from God. A longing is not *strange* to God then. It was not a mankind thing only. We were made from God and for God. If it is in our nature, then it is also in God's nature. In-Love is a beautiful thing. It is a feeling that God knows. God wanted the companionship of man. He longed for someone to love Him and come to Him *willingly.* For this reason, He created us and gave us *free* wills! Now He *longs* for us to choose *Him.* When we stray from God, we long to come back into His presence. The same thing goes for God. He longed so much for us to come back to Him that He gave His Son Jesus—everything He had to give—that we might be reconciled to Him. He *longs* for us to come back into His presence.

This type of love and intensity should be given *back* to God. We should not be *ashamed* to love Him with *all that we are and all that we've got.* Look, God made us physical beings, so need and loneliness on a *physical level* must be satisfied.

That means we need someone *physical* to see, someone *physical* to touch. Hence God created Eve and gave Adam the physical parts he needed for consummation.

Loneliness on both the spiritual and physical levels had to be satisfied—the loneliness for God's presence and the loneliness for a physically befitting companion. Loneliness is, indeed, both a physical and spiritual thing.

Mating is an interchange on the physical, mental, and spiritual levels. Two spirits and two bodies coming together as one truly defines unity. Mating is usually used to describe the fulfillment reached on a physical level when in love. The Bible says that the two lovers become "one." Since mating is more than just a bodily function, Jesus recommended that marriage should be for a lifetime. It should be the mating of minds throughout two people's lifetimes.

Some Pharisees came to Jesus and sought to trick Him. They asked, "'Is it right for a man to divorce his wife for any reason he chooses?' Jesus answered, 'Surely you have read in the scriptures: When God made the world, "He made them male and female," and God said, "So a man will leave his father and mother and *be united* with his wife. And the two people will become *one* body." So there are not two, but one. God has joined the two together, so no one should *separate* them'" (Matt. 19:3-6 NCV). Then he continues, "Moses allowed you to divorce your wives because you refused to *accept* God's teaching, but divorce was not allowed in the beginning" (Matt. 19:8 NCV). God intended marriages to last for a lifetime. He wants married spouses to *cleave* to one another.

Now, let's look at the similarities of cleaving to your spouse and cleaving to God. "Thou shalt fear the Lord thy God; Him shalt thou serve, and to Him shalt thou cleave, and swear by His name" (Deut. 10:20). Sin brought *distortion* and *debasement* into the world.

This polluted and affected *everything*. A well-known man of God once said that sin is not necessarily a matter of lying, stealing, killing, or being immoral, but it's basically an *attitude*. It is going one's independent way, a lack of relationship or fellowship with God—falling short of what He has entrusted to us. Sin often manifests itself as self-centeredness, an attitude of active rebellion against God or passive indifference to Him.

Now God's heartthrob is for us. So much so that satan's philosophy could easily be stated as "the only way to get to God *is* through man. This is the only thing that can *hurt* Him." How very true! It wasn't lucifer making trouble in heaven that was hurting God. He dealt swiftly with that by kicking lucifer out. It was lucifer's interference with mankind, God's loved ones, that *hurt* God. This is what made God *humble*. He humbled Himself, *emptied* Himself on the cross. (See Philippians 2:6-8.) God *literally* gave His all so that mankind might *live*, might be *reconciled* back to Him. How strange, how humble, how exciting!

God dreams of us? He dreamed of us even before we were created. If someone said He is *sentimental* about us, that wouldn't be far from the truth! You could also say that God actually dreamed us up. He thought about how He would make us, what He would give us before He set to work. "He hath chosen us in Him before the foundation of the world, that we should be holy and without blame before Him in love: having predestined us into the adoption of His children by Jesus Christ to Himself, according to the good pleasure of His will" (Eph. 1:4-5).

I love the New Century Version of the Bible, which says in Ephesians 1:9 "This was what God *wanted* and He *planned* to do it through Christ. His *goal* was to carry out His plan when the right time came." Wow! My Creator was dreaming about me.

Now, some people like to spiritualize things. But let's look at the context. If you wanted to express that God wanted us and planned for us, would you say, "I *spiritually* want this?" Would you say, "I spiritually *love* you, Annie?" Of course not; you would simply say, "I love you, Annie." If you wanted a certain pair of shoes, you wouldn't say, "I want these shoes *spiritually*." No, you would simply say, "I want these shoes."

So, simply put, God wanted us and planned for us. We don't go around trying to dissect the feelings of God. Another thing to note is that we are *naturally* spiritual people. Let's stop saying, "God is Spirit, and we are human." We are alike. God's got a soul, you know. He's like you and I are. He says, "But if any man draw back, My *soul* shall have no pleasure in him" (Heb. 10:38).

The Divine Mind Reader

God knows about telepathy! He knows our hearts' cry; He answers us even *before* we call. He knows our *every* desire, our thoughts, and our heartbeat. He knew Adam's thoughts. He was definitely and is definitely *in love* with us. Remember how He knew Adam was lonely even though Adam didn't say anything? Only a lover of the soul would have the ability to read our secret thoughts. Remember, Adam had never seen Eve before. He didn't even know what he wanted. But when God brought Eve to Adam, Adam was delighted and exclaimed, "This is indeed bone of my bone and flesh of my flesh!" (See Genesis 2:23.)

Yes, God thinks about us. He *laughs*. "He that sitteth in the heavens shall laugh" (Ps. 2:4). Jesus *cried* (see John 11:35). Jesus had sympathy and joy. He had compassion. God can *grieve*. Genesis 6:5-6 says, "The Lord saw that the wickedness of man was great in the earth, and that every intent of the thoughts of his heart was only evil continually. And the Lord was sorry that He had made man on the earth, and He was *grieved* in His heart" (NKJV). God, however, is not always moved by emotions—the emotions of His heart— whether you call that "spiritual emotion" or "godly emotion." He is moved by His word and His word is love, *love, love, love.*

Righteous love produces righteous jealousy. Jealousy can be produced when a person has an *intensity* of emotion. You don't feel jealousy for something you are not possessive of or obsessed about. Jealousy can be felt for what is rightfully or wrongfully yours. When a beloved person is taken by another individual, you might feel jealous that the beloved's attention is no longer directed your way.

It should be noted that the object of jealousy need *not* be a beloved. It can be a mere acquaintance you have an intense obsession about. This person or thing may not even be rightfully yours. There can be an envious jealousy, and there can be a jealousy that is unjustified. This would be in regard to something or someone who does not rightfully belong to you but whom you claim.

But we thank God that we *belong* to Him in truth, and more than that, we are His *beloved* and so have the ability to grieve Him. We had the ability to grieve God so much that He acted on this grief once. He destroyed the whole earth with a great flood. Wiped it out! Wow! He is certainly a jealous God and He guards His own. That's the whole complexity of being in love.

He would also give others in exchange for your life! He said, "Since thou wast precious in My sight, thou hast been honourable, and I have loved thee: therefore will I give men for thee, and people for thy life" (Isa. 43:4). He wiped out *all* the armies of Egypt when they were chasing the Israelites at the Red Sea. Unimaginable? No, it isn't. He's in love and bound to go to extraordinary lengths to save those He passionately loves.

Let us always remember that the apostle Paul instructed husbands to love their wives like Christ loved the church and gave *His life* for the church. The giving of life is the *ultimate* sacrifice of love. "Husbands, love your wives, even as Christ also loved the church, and gave Himself for it…that He might present it to Himself a glorious church, not having spot, or wrinkle, or any such thing; but that it should be holy and without blemish" (Eph. 5:25,27).

Husbands are to present their wives *like* Christ is to present the church. The similarity between the two is amazing! I strongly believe that wives should love their husbands, too. Some people would say wives should *respect* and *submit* to their husbands first and foremost. And husbands should strictly *love* their wives! But I believe this, a woman cannot truly be submissive unless she is in love with her husband. She commands her bodily submission and respect through love. Only if this comes from her heart can it be genuine. Jesus said, "If you love Me, keep My commandments [*obey* Me]" (John 14:15 NKJV). In other words if you, the Church, *love* Me then obey Me, keep My commandments. The Church (Bride) should *love* the Bridegroom (Christ) to be able to give of herself (to have the *ability to submit and obey*). Love should be mutual, not one-sided. Adam saw something he wanted in Eve, and Eve saw that she *was made for* Adam. There had to have been mutual feeling, or neither would have been pleased with the other. Love and obey. Love is obedience. They *walk* hand in hand. God says that if we love Him, we will obey him. There is no mystery here, just simple truths.

Jesus loved the Father so much that He was able to *submit* to the Father and shout, "Not My will, but Yours, be done" (Luke 22:42 NKJV). He loved the Father enough to be made the *sacrifice* for sin. His love for the Father made Him able to bear the turning away of God's face on the cross when He cried out, "My God, My God, why have You forsaken Me?" (Matt. 27:46 NKJV). The love He had for the Father was great enough that it poured down upon us when He pleaded in Luke 23:34, "Father forgive them; for they know not what they do" as His hands and feet were nailed to the cross. *He loved, He obeyed, He submitted.*

Now, whether you are married or single, you should remind yourself that you are the *temple* of the Holy Spirit. He dwells *in* you. This is God being *in love*! An "indwelling" is more *potent* than any operation from the outside. It's beautiful that He's living *in* you. That's the *ultimate* love, the ultimate! You are "one spirit" with Him. His Spirit witnesses in *your* spirit that you are the child of God. *His Child.* (See Romans 8:16.)

Another beautiful thought about how much God loves us is that He is in love with us *as much as* He is with Jesus! Jesus said, "You *loved them* just as much as You *loved Me*" (John 17:23 NCV). What greater love can we ask for? It's equally amazing that Jesus, knowing *how much* God loved us, was *not jealous* of such great love. God loves us as much as He loves Jesus! I cannot fully grasp it. However, Jesus, knowing *this,* left all His glory in heaven and became a man. He learned obedience as He was scorned, beaten, and put to death by the very people He had created. And He did this because He loves us *just as passionately* as His Father does. (See John 15:9.) It's humbling to know that God showered such love on us through Jesus and the Holy Spirit. The Holy Spirit dwells in us, guides us, guards us, and sees us through this life. Let's stay *in love* with God, for He deserves it. He asks for it. Let us love Him with intensity and work toward being in love with Him at all times, just as He is with us!

The secret to staying *in love* with Him is to *remain* in His presence. For in His presence there is an influence, an inference of spirits. He says you should love Him with all of your heart, your mind, your soul, and your might. (See Mark 12:30.) Doesn't that mean you should love Him with your emotions? Don't be ashamed to *cry* before Him, love Him like a lover, with the *giving* of yourself and *all* you've got.

Remember this: there is edification, a feeding, within His presence that brings wisdom and fulfillment far beyond your knowledge. Above all, it is a love full of intensity and compassion. It is enduring. It never fails. You can stay *in love* with Him (in His presence) for as long as you want. And this should be forever!

Loving

Some people are very cautious and protective when it comes to loving. Others are given to promiscuity and fall in love with such carelessness that they miss out on the whole beautiful concept of loving. Still others term love as *"dangerous."* In the first instance, God created all *types* of love.

The Greek word *phileo* refers to the type of love between friends, brothers and sisters and other relatives, and the general public. You could say it is a platonic type of love relationship. Parents have it for their children. It is shared by friends and can even be used to describe the love we have for our pet animals. (See Proverbs 12:10.)

The Greek word *eros* refers to the type of love exchanged between lovers—husbands and wives. This is an erotic passion and desire.

The Greek word *agape* is more simply known as God's kind of love. We should have this type of love for everyone we encounter, whether we are married or single. You might call this the *all-consuming love*, which in itself is sufficient. Agape is an *act of will* as well as an act from the heart.

Notice that God creates positive emotions *not* negative ones. Bearing this in mind should comfort you and give direction to your love life. Now, let's take a look at these three types of love and see how they play out.

Eros, at most times, cannot be prevented between interacting adult males and females. It's an emotion of love that most everyone has felt strongly at one time or another. This type of love can be positive if channeled positively. After all, it's what you do with the emotions that matters. Still, many people think of *eros* as the only emotion that can be used destructively. But *phileo* has been used wrongly as well. People lie to their friends, cheat and spite their family members, and hold thoughts of malice and revenge.

They do all these things, yet they love their friends and family members. And what about the great *agape* love? We often abuse it. We ought to love God deeply, with all we've got. And yet, we grieve and hurt Him, both deliberately and by omission in the rush to have our own way.

I strongly believe that *phileo* and *eros* are both engulfed in *agape*. *Eros* derives more bodily pleasure, *phileo* more emotional, and *agape* more spiritual. It is the measure of these pleasures, which compartment—spirit, soul, or body—they fit into, that makes us vulnerable to abusing them (spirit—*agape*, soul—*phileo*, body—*eros*). And when one is used improperly, it affects all the others.

The person who loves the Lord deeply must pass through all the phases of loving Him—as a lover, as a friend, and as His child. The times you sought His presence to please and worship Him and the times you were *ultra*-sensitive to His voice were periods of spiritual *eros*. When you knew God as your companion, the one you laughed with and told the silly things of your heart to, the one with whom you shared your dreams, this was *phileo* love. It is *agape* love that assures you that you cannot be separated from your heavenly Father. (See Psalm 91:1, Romans 8:38-39.) By the way, know that loving God is *eternal* in every form.

Loving in any mode is costly. It demands a price. Nothing *comes* free even if it is given freely. Loving is a *sacrifice* of one's self, time, and sometimes possessions. Energy and effort must be spent for loving to succeed. If not, it won't take *root*. Anything done carelessly will go in the same manner. It never pays to take love and attention for *granted*. Because loving is sensitive to touch, hearing, and sight, care must be taken to address it with sensitivity. Love is like a gentle dove. It is the Holy Spirit who readily comes to mind when I think and talk of love. He is the *embodiment* of love's power and grace. Sensitive, quick to forgive, and powerful in defense, this is love.

The saying that many oceans cannot drown love applies to the Holy Spirit. I believe the ability to love *anybody* is possible when you love God and the Holy Spirit. He gives you the ability to love and forgive. With the Holy Spirit you are able to love without destroying yourself and without struggle. You are capable of loving again, no matter how hurtful you have become. Insensitive or cynical? Do not fear love. It is the true meaning to life. A bit of love *shown* destroys all manner of evil and darkness. God, our Father, is the one who pours this love into our hearts. Love has substance.

Loving your friends (*phileo* love) demands sensitivity to their moods and needs. A friend *in need* is a friend *indeed*. Don't insult your friends with lip service. They depend on you. You can never be an island unto yourself. One day you will need their company and help, or even their experience and advice. Whether you are the soft, sensitive type that gets hurt easily or the tough, self-sufficient type that seldom admits hurt, you need good friends. It is only in loving and appreciating a friend that you can possibly learn how to love and appreciate a spouse.

Physical passion (*eros* love) demands the response of the body as well as the strings it tugs in your heart. It asks a lot of your *visible emotion*. Body *chemistry* begins to flow and *reactions* set in. This is the only place you should seriously "check" yourself. Just the same, this love should be looked at from the angle of its good qualities as well. It makes you *more* sensitive, *willing* to please, and willing to sacrifice all at any cost, your spirit, soul, and body, if need be.

It would help to note that in actuality, love in whatever *form* demands that you give all of *yourself*. For *eros*, it is the amount of visible emotion it takes. The emotions ignite and spark chain reactions throughout the body, lighting it up. What can you do? It is love! And you are a love child from God, so smile. You should use this type of love to become a stronger and wiser person. It won't knock you off your feet because you understand what is happening. You learn to see this as a positive emotion with symptoms that come and go. You won't let your body run away with you, because you know you control your body; it doesn't control you.

Remember, you are a *new creation* by the shedding of the blood of the Lamb, Jesus, which means that all things are subject to Him and the Holy Spirit, even the erotic emotion! You will treat it the way you treat other emotions, that is, from the *inner renewed* man. You are renewed in your mind by the *word* of God. Listen to *worship songs* and *stay in the presence* of the Holy Spirit, and you will defeat *any* negative desire.

You do not move by sight or by feelings. (These have always applied to you, even before you fell in love as a Christian.) So continue to live in the same way! You are moved *by* God. The laws of God do *not* change simply because you are in love. No! If all "loves" are positive, then the laws of God (which are positive as well) should still be followed, applied, and obeyed. It would be wrong to step out of line (not obey the positive laws of God) for a positive emotion, feeling, or love that God Himself has created and constituted. If they are not applied, your hedges would crumble and a snake would come in and bite you!

The Book of Proverbs says, "Keep thy heart with all diligence; for out of it are the issues of life" (Prov. 4:23). "Affections" here can imply love, when it comes from the heart. Guarding your heart means being careful how you love and it's consequences and results. The results *should* be positive. If not, don't even *think* about getting into such a relationship. It is equivalent to a swine trampling you and your treasures. Be warned. It will happen if you let down your hedges! You will be pursued and trampled to the very dust. (See Matthew 7:6.)

Love is a treasure—a gem. Don't throw it away. Don't live in your soul realm. You are a new person, a spirit. *Eros* stirs the soul realm when it sparks bodily desires. Switch into your spirit. Change the source; make it deeper, more fruitful for the kingdom.

Direct it to come from the springs of living water pouring from your spirit man. As a spirit being, born again of the Father, talk to your soul and *demand* that the soul and emotion obey you. Say to your soul, "I *love* Annie, but I will not *defile* her because I am love!" Love does not defile. Hand yourself over to God and let the Holy Spirit slip through.

Remember, too, *eros* is not the *only* love. God demands that you love a friend deeply. A good Christian friend *can* lay down his life for another. Consider, too, the love of a parent for a child. The list goes on and on. Every kind of love is good. It is the measure you give to it and the positive things you do with it that matter. The key to the *success* of love is *loving* God and putting Him *before* everything else. That way, no matter the outcome of the relationship, you would be a better person for it. *Make sure you put Him—God—first!*

I wish everyone could catch this vision and stop worrying about love, sex, relationships, or marriage. Anxiety about your marital status is not productive. Instead, live fully the life you have now.

Union

Think about it in this way. We breathe air into our lungs to live. This is a union. The air goes into our lungs to make us function and live. It is as simple as the union of our hearts and minds (as simple as the union of our sexual parts, too). This is living, an *interaction*. We laugh and cry because something or someone caused us to. We interact and react to circumstances and situations around us. These are expressions of love *and exchange*, a mating: sex in its most "natural state." God made us for exchange. All these remind me of how God, Jesus, and the Holy Spirit are interwoven all together with us. One mind, one goal, one purpose, to the glory of God our Father, the Creator. We are referred to as His Bride and shall meet for a *marriage* banquet. All these are expressions of our union. Can you now understand? (See Matthew 22:30, Romans 12:5, Ephesians. 4:3-5.)

Married or single, all have interactions of their own, unions brought about by the mating of minds, hearts, things, and circumstances.

As we've said, God is the *originator* of unions, and He has given this attribute to us. These unions come from *love* and demand that we get the *best* out of our friendships and relationships. Let's enjoy them for as long as we live and make them meaningful and worthy of emulation. Some friendships or relationships don't last for a variety of reasons. Go out and make *clean, honest* friends. There are honest friendships out there and Christian activities that *nurture* these healthy relationships. Choose *healthy* Christian activities that help you to keep your hormones from running away with you! Love your friends the way God wants you to love them; equally let these friends be those who have noble intentions and are of good character. Give yourself this chance and learn from it. This approach to love is a good thing that you should have no reason to fear. All *good* things (like these) come from God. (See James 1:17.) As God's chosen ones, filled with a *new spirit*, the Holy Spirit, let's love in the ways God says we should.

2

Spiritual Feeding

How we flow in His presence is determined by the food we eat. Like the body, the spirit man needs feeding. Try good, quiet Christian music (praise and worship songs). This type of music will *feed* your spirit and help you grow. Quiet moments, solitude, and silence are equally necessary for growth, maturity, and survival in our world filled with noise and distractions.

The starter food, however, for the spirit is the Word of God. The *authentic* Word of God is found only in the Bible.

Careful Consumption

Outside of the Bible, you must be careful of what you consume. Avoid videos and books that teach violence and ungodly sex. Stay away from those things that are full of gossip and slander, backbiting or rumor seeking. These will affect you. The company you keep and the atmosphere in the places you go matter a lot, too. (See First Corinthians 15:33.) *Learn* to be in the presence of the Holy Spirit. Ask Him to take control, and He will—if you *allow* Him to. Ask Him what *He wants* to do, not what *you want* to do. (See Philippians 2:13.) The amazing thing is that as you go about doing the will of God, the Father, He *will* give you the desires of your heart as well. (See Psalm 37:4.) In following your own will, you will only be chasing the wind. Never achieving, constantly frustrated, always pursuing.

The most effective ways to be in the Spirit and remain in the presence of God are to listen to Christian worship songs, read the Bible, and listen to His words. As you consistently do these things, prayer and thanksgiving will begin to bubble up from your heart, bursting forth, fresh and pure at all times. Learn to be *church,* just you and the Holy Spirit. Your personal edification is not limited to the assembly of the brethren, so encourage yourself to seek the Lord *personally.* There is one caution here. Make sure you do not deceive yourself into thinking you are fellowshiping with God the Father, when you are *actually* backsliding. You will know when you are backsliding when you have no *desire* whatsoever to be with other Christians. If you have not learned this unique, personal fellowship just between you and the Holy Spirit, then make sure you are in fellowship with other believers. The assembly of the brethren will serve to encourage, uplift, and comfort you. The Lord speaks in the assembly of His people. (See Hebrews 10:25.)

It is necessary, however, for those busy in the ministry, such as church workers and other staff, to set aside quiet times with the Holy Spirit—just the two of you. If you are always involved with activities and find out you don't have time for your *own personal* time with the Holy Spirit, you must do something about it. If you find yourself preaching, teaching, or working during the services or assemblies, you will soon find yourself hungry and resentful due to the time consumed and the work pressure. Misunderstandings can build. You need time to worship and praise God and be fed yourself. Otherwise, you will be surprised at the skeleton you can become.

Another thing is "group anointing" that streams from working in a group. When this is removed, without your own *fresh* fellowship with the Lord, you will be totally empty, naked, and without any covering anointing. This really shouldn't be. Your covering should always be the Lord Jesus (on the "first layer"). Do not be weary. Keep up the good fight, and have courage. You are dear to God's soul. Personally spend time with the *Person* of the Holy Spirit.

Remember, dear ones, you are *one* with the Holy Spirit. Establish it in your heart and mind that you and the Holy Spirit *live* together. If you haven't asked Him into your life, ask Him now—please! Don't you understand that the body you wear is also worn by the Holy Spirit? Put it firmly into your subconscious that you are *not* your own. You have been bought with a precious price. The death, the life, the blood of Jesus was shed that you may live. (See First Corinthians 6:19-20.)

Be alert in your spirit so that nothing takes you by surprise. Remember that satan is a deceiver and don't be caught in his trap. Don't dismiss things; remember how the evil one comes. He may change tactics, but he is still gunning for the same thing. Be alert and aware of the things that happen in your life. Watch out for the subtlety of satan in your dealings. You and the Holy Spirit make an *unbeatable* team.

Making the Effort

Along with being alert, make efforts to be with the Holy Spirit every *second,* so that being tuned in to Him becomes a habit as *normal* as breathing. Don't *let go* and allow the wind to carry you. *Letting go* refers to the times you've said, "I'm drying up again, but that's all right." Or maybe you've thought, "I know I'm drying up, but I'll be fresh again soon. These things come and go." This is a *wrong* attitude! Don't allow yourself to go dry. Too much *fluctuation* is not good for you spiritually. You should work to reach a level of maturity where you are stable and growing. Then you can make up your mind and stand by it.

Making the *effort* to do something about your situation is a *positive* step. Make those small efforts to be with the one you love, the Holy Spirit. Set aside time to seek the presence of Jesus. It's the same principle that applies to your physical relationships. Little efforts like talking to Him in the depths of your sadness or constant weakness are important. In fact, any effort at all to be with Him matters a lot.

There are also areas where you should *not* be directing your efforts. God does not want you to rely on your own efforts and struggles. You cannot make it with your own strength or self-will. You can only do so by His spirit. "Not by might nor by power, but by My Spirit, says the Lord of Hosts" (see Zech. 4:6 NKJV). Let go and let God.

Put all your efforts toward becoming all He wants you to be. Ask Him to help you learn when to let go of your efforts and let Him handle things. Your efforts and His control should, however, *intermingle* with one another. They should go hand in hand.

The time to act is when you have grieved Him *deliberately*. The truth is that we Christians sometimes deliberately sin against the Holy One. Maybe because we know He forgives or because we take Him for *granted*. We should be ashamed of this irresponsibility. Deliberate sin is saying, in more ways than one, that God cannot trust us or take us seriously. In this way, you limit the trust the Holy Spirit has in you.

It may amaze you, but He does depend on you to understand Him, not just to carry out His will but also to care for Him as He cares for you and to trust Him. It's not just your spirit He needs; He needs your thoughts, as well. No wonder He asks that you meditate on the *fruit* of the *Spirit,* the things that are pure. (See Philippians 4:8-9.) Your mind is the *outlet* for your spirit. It is how the two of you *interact*. Your spirit is His electric *current* and wire. Your mind and your intellect He uses for *His* expressions. You've got to express Him anyway, don't you? And how do you do it?

Through your soul! Your body is His, too, the vehicle for the *physical* manifestation of the Spirit. Do you know that in the *eyes* of the Spirit, not only do our faces glow (like Moses), but our bodies, too? (See Exodus 34:29,35.) Virtue flows out of us to reach others, like Jesus. The Holy Spirit dwells in us and is with us. Hooray!

God intended from the *beginning* that we should be one with Him. "He who is joined to the Lord is one Spirit with Him" (1 Cor. 6:17 NKJV). Now, what would you do if you offended or grieved someone you knew? Wouldn't you go to the aggrieved person and say you're *sorry*? Would you wait for the aggrieved person to come to you? If this person does not come, would you not persist to win back the friendship? After all, the offended person has the right to stay back, take time to get over the hurt, and forgive you!

The principle is the same with the Holy Spirit. Give the Holy Spirit the *same* understanding you would give a human friend. When you sin deliberately, go to Him and *ask* for His forgiveness. You grieved the One who paid a great price to set you free and be with you, for the Holy Spirit and Jesus are one. What touches the Son touches the Holy Spirit and the Father. They were in agreement concerning Christ's coming, His death, and the coming of the Holy Spirit to earth. (See John 14:16-18; John 16:13-15; Hebrews 10:7; Colossians 1:15.) Anyone who touches you touches God the Father, God the Son, and God the Holy Spirit, our triune God. (See John 14:23.) We are *all* bound together.

So persist and do those small things He loves. Bare your soul to Him. Do something! Resist the urge to relax and say, "Oh, He will come back, because He always does!" That is inconsiderate of you and not becoming of your relationship with Him. It will amaze you to discover the totality of your inconsideration of the Holy One. You may grieve for your inconsideration. Don't take that chance.

This inconsideration and grievance could lead to a long separation from the Holy Spirit, thus making way for the evil one to toss you up or down. Leaving things unresolved only makes them worse. Do you still expect Him to come to you, after so long? You did not treat the Holy Spirit with consideration or give Him the honor He deserves, even the honor given a dear friend. Sooner than later, it happens. Self creeps in—slowly and deliberately. Then the devil and distractions cripple you, and you cave in.

At this junction, friend, it is time to cry out to Him for help! Don't just sit there. Cry out and call on Him now! Don't let hurt, guilt, or grudges hold out on you. The *most* important thing is for you to retain the relationship you have had with the Holy gentle One. He is waiting.

Self-Control

God has given us Christians the fruit of the Spirit, and these are love, joy, peace, longsuffering, kindness, goodness, faithfulness, gentleness, and self-control. (See Galatians 5:22-23.) You have the same ability to produce the fruit of the Spirit in your life as an evangelist or pastor has. It doesn't matter if you are married or single.

Now, this is for those who are *unmarried*. In First Corinthians 7:5, we read that the husband and wife who abstain from intercourse due to fasting and prayer should come together again *after* they completed this commitment. They exercise *self-control* while apart! You can argue that it is better to marry, because the times we are living in are evil times. I want to assure you that from time immemorial, sin has always been there. Multiple sins are recorded in the Bible. From there comes the account of the notorious Sodom and Gomorrah. (See Genesis 19:4-9.)

The key word found in Galatians 5:23 is *self-control*. Don't think because married couples have a companion that they don't ever exercise this. In First Thessalonians 4:4-5, it says, "Each of you should know how to live with your wife in a holy and honorable way, not with a lustful desire, like the heathen who do not know God" (GNT). The New Living Translation says "Not in lustful passion like the pagans who do not know God and his ways." So, there is a self-control practiced by married couples.

It is quite true that the way to live a godly life *lies* in Christ, who came to earth as a *man,* not as an angel or anything else! Let's not lose sight of that. The Bible says that the *answer* lies in Christ, *not* in marriage, ministry, post, or position. Marriage was given to men and women, but it is possible to have a satisfying, fulfilled life without marrying. Marriage can help or hinder. First Corinthians 7:29-35 includes this instruction, "Let even those who have wives be as though they had none" (NRSV). This does not mean neglect your wife or family. (See First Timothy 5:8.) Instead, it means you should stay as *available* as possible for the Lord. That means that those of you who are *totally* free (unmarried) can do so much more. You have no excuse. The day of the Lord should not come to you like a thief in the night and meet you unprepared!

3
EMOTIONS

Emotions coming from *self* are unreliable. They are as change-able as *moods* and, therefore, should not be trusted. One of the most difficult tangles to overcome is emotion's tentacles once you have *given in*. You will be able to stay more rational once you have looked at this topic closely and critically.

Emotions come from the soul realm. The soul consists of your will, emotions, and intellect. Emotion, however, often gets the most attention because it is hard to suppress. It is the outlet of one's soul. Expression is that internal response that you *exhibit* from either a *disturbance* within you or an *external stimulus*.

The first question to ask is, what are those things you take into your soul? Be cautious about these. You will definitely *react* to them positively or negatively. What are the things you *see*; what are the things you *read*? They will come back to you recorded in the form of thoughts and take root. Your response or reaction is then expressed *through* your emotions.

When thoughts come subconsciously and subtly and you *submit* to their onslaught, your emotions will respond accordingly. The rea-son most people are not able to control their emotional lives is be-cause they *do not* control their *thought life*. Negative, errant thoughts may not be totally quenched, but they can be *controlled*. Knowing this allows you to make an *effort* to check your thought pattern. The only way emotion can grip you is through your mind and thoughts!

Be *realistic* enough to check your thoughts and also your confessions (that is, what you say). Remember, it is easy to become ensnared by the words that come out of your mouth. (See Proverbs 6:2.) When you admit you hate someone, you will eventually begin to hate the person. The same goes when you admit you love someone! These are confessions, *statements*. As long as you want to control your emotions, check your thought life and seal your mouth! Watch what you say. You have the ability to do so. It is a struggle sometimes, especially if you *desire* such thoughts. But life's spice is full of pain, hurt, and joy. You must be wise. Proverbs says, "Guard your affections for there flows the issues of life" (Prov. 4:23, author's paraphrase).

It does not pay to live anxiously or worry constantly. This is futile. It is better to save yourself the energy you waste when you let your emotions take an upper hand. Emotions are *irrational* by nature. They are not realistic and cannot always be subjected to *reason*. Life thrives on facts, and to survive, you must learn to keep things in balance. It is better if the emotion is released at the *right things* and at the *right time,* rather than being allowed to demand its own space. This is where your intellect comes in.

Balancing the head and the heart is typically more difficult for women than for men. For the most part, men are able to keep their emotions at bay as they think things through, while women have a tendency to act with their hearts. That changes, though, when men and women are subject to the influence of the Holy Spirit. There are times the heart should rule the head, and others when the head should be in charge. It is not by might, nor by reason, neither by will power that you can conquer emotion, but by the *spirit*. (See Zechariah 4:6.)

It is better to have *knowledge* of what has crippled you time and time again. Examine it and know *how* to handle it. It is not necessary or essential that you hate emotion. Emotion is beautiful in itself. It is, in fact, the most beautiful expression of a human soul, a longing, a yearning that is most marvelous when shared. But it is necessary to control it. This is the *mark* of a strong character and a responsible, mature personality. Checking your emotion matures you, whether that emotion is anger, sadness, disappointment, or the thoughts of a loved one. Love should consist of *substance, quality, or value*. Any emotion that is not of substance or any relationship that is not of quality should be rejected.

Remember this: you can have desirous, emotional affiliations with different people. It is absolutely possible! Men often feel this far more than women. They have the capacity of sleeping with different women, or feel like it, all in a short period of time. The mistake here is that people mistake these emotions for love. However, these emotions are not love. When a woman sees the man she loves express emotion toward another woman, she should not panic. On the other hand, a man in a relationship should avoid showing special emotional affiliation to any person other than the woman he truly loves. These expressions can be destabilizing when they are not directed at the person you are committed to!

Another thing is that these emotions can subtly change in intensity to the level of being *in love*, so watch it! Don't let those thoughts crowd you. Let your loving come from a deliberate decision. Love both intellectually (using the head) and emotionally (using the heart). This will become easier with time, interaction, communication, and decisions. This is what I call "sensible irrational loving." *Sensible* because of the head, *irrational* because emotion is involved.

Just remember, you should not dismiss emotion, or the woman in your life will likely be unhappy. But the decision part of the head will make your relationship stronger and steadier.

Emotions can spring from situations as well. The "click" is when two people of the opposite sex meet and there is chemistry between them, of either a platonic or erotic nature. This click will likely take place anytime you see each other, no matter the environment, situation, or people around you. Emotions that spring from this situation will grow when the individuals are in close interaction, close proximity, or become confidants. Emotions and thoughts can be aroused.

Some people go through their lives making this same mistake over and over again and wondering why. They don't realize they could have avoided it. The statement "once bitten, twice shy" is not always true. Once uncontrolled emotions are involved, these individuals often continue to act foolishly.

Feelings are an indication of an emotional onslaught. Avoid those feelings by avoiding proximity to these situations. Don't go and see the other person when your emotions are running high. This is a time to stay away in order to stay safe. Act normally, think normally and rationally. *Make* yourself do so. *Decide to do so.*

Restraining or banning emotions, however, has its dangers and disadvantages. It can *inhibit* some people, causing them to retreat and be withdrawn. It can make an already subdued, quiet person vulnerable to a nervous breakdown or hypertension. To avoid this, simply keep your thoughts in check. Go out, smile, laugh, and do constructive things. Express yourself fully in other meaningful ways, just be sensible and avoid danger! Go ahead and don't let anything eat you up. Nothing is hindering you and nothing should hinder you. This is what we want. Life is for living. Live in safety and be happy.

Another strange way to deal with your emotional side is to love these emotions in themselves. Have no fear of expressing what you feel, without slur or the fear of rejection. If you are rejected, bear it well. Don't let it maim you.

Like loving, emotion should actually be a positive reaction. It is when it is abused that it is destructive. You are the one who determines *whether* your emotions are going to be destructive or not. Someone else can abuse your emotion, but it is you who can positively and personally decide what to do with what you feel!

Expressing emotion in a happy, clean, clear relationship is the best thing possible. It means enhancing a friendship, putting on a smile, and spreading hope in someone's life. Love people *the way* God says to. This is constructive! Even in nonprogressive relationships that have gone sour, you should not despair. Learn from those hurtful relationships so you will be built up in the end. God intends for you to be built up! Emotion consists of your make-up and your essence. Don't be suspicious, cold, and lonely, no matter how much energy has been drained out of you. Turn to God and have a positive outlook toward life.

Christians should, above all, know that we walk not by sight but by faith. Emotions that are from self are *direct links* to what we see and what we feel, but we do not live according to mortal dictates, especially when we know and have an insight into the outcome. God gives us that insight.

Loving God With Your Emotions

We have said that an emotion can be constructive, and, yes, it can be. Emotions are good and constructive when channeled toward a worthy cause. It is God, after all, who gave us these emotions for expression, so we should look at emotion in a good light.

Let's look at this from another angle. God created good things. He created us good. It was sin that brought death, destruction, and perversion to things. Christians ought to be clean-minded people. John 15:3 says, "Ye are clean through the word which I have spoken unto you." We are redeemed people, being conformed to the image of our Creator. Our thoughts and hearts should be pure toward God. To the pure, all things are pure. (See Titus 1:15.) This is how it should be for us! We should not tolerate perversion but have clean minds.

There is also an emotion that stems from the Spirit. The Spirit impresses it on the soul. The Holy Spirit dwells within you and has need for expression, remember? The soul thus expresses these feelings from the spirit man. It is not self- or flesh-centered, nor does it have anything to do with a partner. Rather, it would be doing something *for* a person or a partner. Jesus was moved with compassion and healed the sick. Our emotions in loving God should not be held back.

I do not believe that those who cry when they pray are just emotional and not spiritual! Tears come when something grieves your being or when something touches your heart. Most times, it is a cry from within. David in the Psalms says that his tears drenched his pillows, day and night. (See Psalm 6:6 NKJV.) David was a spiritual man. Some prophets cried out for Israel to repent. They spoke from God's heart. I think people who *feel* are more real than those who don't. To love God is not just faith, and neither is prayer. Rattling off things you don't feel isn't helpful. Praying with your understanding is a feeling and a knowing. Sometimes people need to break down and cry before God. It will not make you less of a person.

Doctors recommend tears. They say tears help release tension. Women are said to live longer than their husbands because they cry and give release to their frustrations, while men tend to store them up. Men are not supposed to cry? How wrong! A contrite heart God will not reject. Who says that tears don't *move* God? Tears from the heart will always move the Almighty. They have spiritual significance. Even Jesus wept. (See John 11:35.) I believe tears can come from your prayers. God says to Hezekiah in Isaiah 38:5, "I have heard thy prayer, I have seen thy tears: behold, I will add unto thy days fifteen years." This was after God had given the prophet Isaiah a prophecy that King Hezekiah would die. God changed the plans because King Hezekiah *cried bitterly*. It is a foolish man who cries when nothing pricks him. God has a soul.

He feels. He says in Hebrews 10:38, "But if any man draw back, my soul shall have no pleasure in him."

Another emotional display is seen in Psalm 2:4, which says, "He that sitteth in the heavens shall laugh." Another emotional display is recorded when Jesus *cried out* in the temple with a loud voice. He used a whip and chased the moneychangers and traders out of the temple. (See Luke 19:45.) Jesus cried when He was told that Lazarus was dead. Jesus was *moved* with compassion—so much so that He healed the multitude. *Moved* is an emotion from within. Jesus, our great anchor, displayed emotion toward us at the cross of Calvary.

Who then are we not to love Him back with this same emotion that He bestowed upon us? Why do we *suppress* our emotions and claim we have none for Him? Loving Him is more than a matter of faith. God, who is a faithful God, was motivated to send the best, Jesus. He died to ransom our souls. It is the *heart* that loves, not faith. Faith, hope, and love, the greatest of these is love. (See 1 Corinthians 13:13 NKJV.) Anything coming from such a pure heart of love is welcome to God. It is precious in His sight. We don't *love* God by faith. We love Him from our hearts.

When you are attuned to the Holy Spirit, your whole essence is sanctified, cleansed for His use! Your whole essence right down to your emotional being is attuned to Him and will line up with Him. It is a whole, *complete,* and total sacrifice. A sweet aroma of yourself. It is of a truth that His people, which we are, shall worship Him in *spirit and in truth.* This is it. Our whole essence, in truth, attuned to Him!

Can you imagine saying you love someone but not showing it with a gesture or an expression? Wouldn't you feel a bit like a fake? Presents, food, gifts, and gestures all have an important place in a relationship.

The Holy Spirit is sensitive and *feels* things. He is *grieved* and thus silenced. He is *sensitive* to words and actions. He is a personality, remember? And there is *no personality* that does not feel. His being grieved is an emotion; His being happy within you until you burst into song is an emotion that you both feel. He, as a personality, is expressing Himself through you. When He withdraws, you are bound to feel dry and empty inside. God created emotions in the soul for a reason: *to be used as the expression for the spirit man.*

Those who are not born again are spiritually dead and have no life. Their spirits have lost the true life. First John 5:12 says, "He that hath not the Son of God hath not life." And so their emotions cannot be *centered* by God. As Christians, don't despise emotions. God has them. God was *angry* with the Israelites in the desert and wanted to wipe them out. That was an emotion. Moses intervened by interceding for the people, and God *refrained.* During Noah's generation, the thoughts and deeds of the people of the world were constantly evil, and God was *sorry* He had made them. He wiped out that generation.

I believe that when you are sensitive to the Spirit, your soul will adjust in order for you to express the Spirit *within* you. You are one spirit with Him. (See First Corinthians 6:17.) Jesus lived like this. You should know when emotion is from the flesh and when it is from the Spirit. Jesus knew when it was self. He said, "Not My will, but thine, be done" (Luke 22:42 NKJV). He wanted the cup to pass from Him in the Garden of Gethsemane. All *throughout* His ministry, He was moved with compassion for people: He fed them, healed them, and raised them from the dead. He had the perfect balance. He was so in tune with God that all He desired was to do the will of God the Father who sent Him. He was *inseparable* from God because He loved God with *all* His heart, His mind, His strength, His essence, His emotions, and all He was.

Once you are in fellowship with the Holy Spirit, constantly being transformed by the *renewing* of your mind by the *Word of God*, you are always on your way up, not down! The whole of your being—spirit, soul, and body—will be quickened by the Holy Spirit who resides in you. (See Romans 8:11.) Virtue and power will flow out from your body and touch people. From your presence, they will feel the presence of God. Moses' face physically shone with the radiance of God after he had talked with God on the mountain for forty days and nights. The Holy Spirit is not restricted to forty days in your life. He resides in you. You should literally light up!

I love watching people who love the Lord cry out in tears, laugh, roll on the floor, jump, etc.—though moderation is important for order in the church. Do you know that the lifting up of your hands is like the expression of tears? It is an expression when you feel like kneeling or prostrating yourself before the Father. It is an expression when you lift your face upward to Him or bow your head. It is an expression when you shout out or whisper a prayer only for Him. These are all expressions of emotion, displays of what and how you feel inside. Tears should not be thought of any differently.

In the privacy of your room, do all you wish to do in order to express your emotions to God—cry, roll, go naked before God. Don't be ashamed to express yourself the way you wish. Sometimes people are hindered because they *restrain* what they feel when praying. Instead of crying, they are more concerned about their makeup or what the people around them might think! Instead of kneeling down before the Holy One or lifting their hands in surrender and release, they let pride rule them. Others refrain because of shyness. Learn to be free in the presence of the Lord. God's presence is the rightful place to freely express your emotions.

There is nothing that does not involve emotion. When you tune in to faith, you tune in to the emotion of faith, the emotions of the spirit, and turn off the emotions and feelings of self. God is a personality and all personalities have emotions! This lets us know we're from God, who has a heart for us, and a heart of love supersedes all things. Love the Lord with all of your heart, mind, strength, and might, all that you are, all that you have. (See Mark 12:30.)

Alone

We sometimes need space, a little time alone to sort things out. Sometimes we seek out an hour or so for these quiet moments. God often chooses these periods of solitude to purify our thoughts and actions as we ponder, reflect, and reconsider our ways. God in His way is trying to bring us to a point of purity. Most of the time people think that holiness is not a possibility in this life. They think, *I can't make it.* Maybe the word *holy* sounds tougher than *purity.* But being pure in mind is being holy as well. Peace of mind brings quietness to a situation. God wants you quiet so He can fill you with Himself. He wants you to slow down from all your activities and let His peace and joy make the difference. It is time you learned to appreciate being alone with Him—just the two of you and nobody else in the whole wide world.

The issue of aloneness is as important as togetherness. Togetherness, for most people, is completeness. But I believe aloneness, solitude, is completeness also. I believe it is a comparative word. "Ye are complete in him" (Col. 2:9-10). You as your whole integral *separate* self. Just you. Completeness implies the *wholeness* and *purity* of your personal mind to God.

It can be said that completeness means perfection. You can definitely achieve this on your own without being attached, engaged, or married! A partner can hinder or help you. Aloneness calls for you to *look within.* That's completeness. The Holy Spirit *indwells you!* You can commune with Him. He is the one who will teach you all things. He is the one who lives in you to make you complete. You see, you cannot divorce purity *from* completeness, regardless of whether you are married or not. You cannot divorce completeness from your aloneness because *as separate as you are*, you're complete in Him! It all goes hand in hand, and this is where God wants to lead you. Not into love affairs here or there.

A perfect illustration is seen in Proverbs 3:6, "In all thy ways acknowledge Him, and He shall direct thy paths." He shall direct your pathway and give you the desires of your heart. The secret is being with the Lord (complete in Him) as you *walk with* Him. Not only will He give you the desires of your heart, but you are *one* spirit with Him. Can you beat that? You are in perfection with Him, *complete* in Him *as* you walk together.

As long as you are restless, you *cannot* make it. So long as you panic or do your own thing and go your own way*, independent* of God's plan for you (married, single, separated, or divorced), you will never fully be *fulfilled*. God wants to be your constant companion, the person you go to for advice and answers to your questions. He is the one you should give your ear to constantly. "Your first." Life is fulfilling while alone, *once* you have the "words of this life." The Bible says, "Go, stand in the temple and speak to the people all the words of this life" (Acts 5:20 NKJV). The words of this life are embedded in God, and this is the essence of life. This essence can be found in the revelations, instructions, and intuitions that come from God. This is *what* will pull down barriers and get you through conflict. Don't chase ghosts or shadows. God will bring the real thing your way. Stay in tune with Him. You are not missing out on anything. That's satan's lie.

There is no guarantee that life will be rosy when you acquire the position you seek or get married. That won't necessarily make your problems vanish! Many people find that when the *fever* of the newly married life or the excitement of that much-sought-after position has worn off, they realize they need His grace and wisdom even more to make their lives a *success*! Why? Because to make *anything* a success requires effort, *dedication*, God's counsel, and *grace*. This same grace is what is required when you are alone. Ask yourself if you have ever appreciated the gift of aloneness. Do you see only a lack of romance or your personal difficulties? Put that aside and walk in the ability He has given you. Think of it this way: should you eventually get married, your commitment will be *till death*. It will be too late to appreciate the gifts of aloneness, so use this time wisely. It is a precious gift entrusted to all men and women at some point or another in their lives.

One of the reasons people don't *understand* this gift is that they are busy using up their days alone *unwisely,* dreaming of a Prince Charming or Snow White, jumping from one love affair to the other, lazing around or partying. They're busy doing nothing. Don't spend your whole life dreaming of and pining over someone you might never meet. The best idea is to spend your moments constructively and productively. The *first* step is to *enjoy* being *alone* with God. After that, you can use your time to appreciate nature, meet new people, develop clean, steady friendships, and pursue a healthy career. Choose friends who share your core beliefs, even if their views might be somewhat different. Try understanding them. Take an interest in them. Don't take them for granted.

Another step is to develop and *maintain* platonic friendships, especially when there is a *rapport*. Strongly resist the temptation to be lovers with anyone until you get married to that person. And when married, don't harbor secret loves in your heart or commit adultery. It soils things. In the end, premarital sex, adultery, or what some people refer to as "flings" will numb your *finer* sensitivity. They hampers the ultimate union of hearts and deep-felt love derived within your relationship. Platonic relationships help *develop* your mind, therefore choose your friends wisely, especially those of the opposite gender. Make the most of constructive friends who can *edify* you. Study what motivates them, what makes them tick—the whys of their character and their ways of reasoning. Know when it's best to drop a friendship and when you should work hard to keep it. This will make you wiser and more mature. For those of you who are married, stay away from old flames you still secretly admire. Don't fool yourself. Adultery is crouching at the door.

Another step to take while you are learning to appreciate your aloneness is to *enjoy your career* or whatever you find yourself doing. I hope you chose a career you love. Are you a nurse, a teacher, secretary, accountant, trader, salesman, student, engineer, doctor? Love your career and do your best by it.

If you aren't in a career you love or a job where you feel God has placed you, think about making a change. Don't move in haste, but begin to work toward moving to something you can feel passionate about, something God has called you to. This normally flows with your natural talent or nature. Remember that this is apart from your communion with God or fellowshiping with Christian brethren. That is basic! A final word for the career individual is this: don't let it *compete* with God. Don't bury your *entire* self in your career. Just do it right and enjoy it.

When you are alone and content, you will not be bored. Contentment *does not* bring boredom. Boredom *seeks* contentment. Boredom generates a *need* for *excitement*. That's why a bored person goes out to party, drink, and look for entertainment. The kind of excitement boredom generates is *not* fulfilling. It fades in the long run. Then you're back where you started—with a loneliness only Jesus can fill. If excitement comes where contentment *has* been *reached,* however, it will linger on, and when the excitement fades, contentment will *still* remain. Thank God for Jesus. Contentment received from the things of God will last forever because they are of eternal value.

Life is worth living, regardless of your marital status. You can be respected and worthy of great responsibilities. You can be an example to the Christian brethren and society at large.

Temptations

People are different, so it makes sense that there would be a wide range of *different* desires and temptations. (See James 1.) But the most common temptations revolve around *money* and *relationships*.

Many people are tempted to love the wrong person. "Wrong" refers to someone who is not "suitable." For many Christian women, this is caused by *anxiety* triggered by age and finances. Often a woman feels all the good men are married, so she settles for a third-rate mate who is not worthy of her heart, or who is not in agreement with her standards or morals. A man can make similar mistakes and tie himself to an unsuitable woman.

These situations could easily have been *avoided* had they kept their eyes open and their ears attuned to the Holy Spirit. Of course, these people made their beds and so must lie in them. Because they are God's children, He will see them through, but still they will have to pay a high price. What God can and will do is to help you endure your situations and deal with your problems, if you allow Him to.

What we ought to note is that there are some decisions and actions that result in consequences no matter how much we would wish to turn back the clock. God can and will forgive, but the price for those hasty, unwise decisions will have to be paid. Though God forgave him, David paid a price for taking Uriah's wife. He lost his son.

Cain killed Abel and became a vagabond. Jonah hid from God and was swallowed by a fish. Don't think that was a simple punishment! First he was thrown into the raging sea and then swallowed by a giant ocean creature. Once he realized he was still alive, he must have wondered if he would ever get out of there. He certainly must have wondered where the fish would take him. When he finally did get out, his skin peeled off from the acid in the whale's stomach. Jonah's punishment was *necessary* to bring him back to God's *focal* point. While he was suffering in the belly of the whale, God was preparing him, renewing his *mind* for the work ahead.

This is what it means to be chastised by God. Your misfortunes, mistakes, and mishaps are sometimes lessons you need to learn to ensure that next time, you are more careful about your choices and actions and less likely to take things for granted. Chastisement will not kill you. It will make you a more mature, responsible, and wise person.

Yes, even though God is faithful to forgive, we often must suffer the consequences of our actions. Once the tape has started rolling, we have to see it through to the end. We reap what we have sown. He can intervene and tide us over and, hallelujah, He is faithful to forgive. That is the *best* part—the part that matters. God has wiped away the record of our sins and given us a clean slate, so we can face the world, whatever comes, with boldness. Don't let anxiety or pressure bend you to *compromise* your standards. You will live to regret it. If not now, later. Little drops of water will fill a bucket.

The other temptation is money. Once we start *grabbing for more*, the *desire* for material assets continues to *increase*. Now we are tempted to compromise even more for money. Who are we kidding? It might seem like its working for a while, but eventually we will have to pay for our actions and decisions. This is the subtlety of the evil one. It is a slow process that starts in the mind. Once we give an inch in our minds by entertaining certain thoughts, we have already given *access* to the devil. He has been here on this earth longer than we have. Do you remember how he outwitted our forefathers? You simply cannot outwit him with your own reasoning. It is better not to take the money or start anything at all! Especially if we feel a *check* in our spirit. It does not matter if it's a well-to-do brother, lukewarm sister, Christian, Muslim, or pagan. If God says no to you, it's a no.

It is important to state here that we should not follow anybody's pattern of life, *as pertaining to* what God has originally instructed or revealed to us. *That's our blueprint*—His voice and His instruction. In terms of relationship, you *will* pay when you derail. Do you know that time spent with the person you shouldn't be with is payment and *defilement* of some sort? That minute or hour you didn't *want* to spend with him or her? The talking that *didn't* edify, the company (then platonic) *is* payment? The corruption of your mind has indeed *started* ever so subtly. Always know that God can fulfill your dreams and desires no matter how romantic, creative, or ambitious you are. Believe it, and you will not lack for anything. He will change things and give you things in time—sometimes sooner than you expect.

Now ladies, don't you know that inner beauty is *far better* and worthier than the outward splendor of words, clothing, jewelry, and all? God, the Most High, prizes you highly. You have found favor in His eyes. Don't let Him down because of your desires or some shortcomings! Bless people with your money but don't be foolish. You are storing up treasures in heaven. There is a bank there. Invest there more often than you invest down here. Of a truth, Jesus said that where your treasures are, that's where your heart will be also. (See Matthew 6:21.) Let's direct our hearts then to heaven and put our most valuable treasures there. Compared to our lives and the people we love, it's just money. In Heaven there are no moths and thieves can't break in. There are no disappointments, worries, or anxieties. Don't be weary in well doing, for in due season you will reap (see Gal. 6:9). The most sophisticated weapons of satan are not found in direct attacks (demons, oppression, witches, etc.) but in *subtlety*. It is the subtle way he has *of getting us away from the things of God*. It starts with the slow wearing away of your strength in Christ brought on by a habit or an area of neglect—most likely the type that would take you years to quit, while its tentacles are being hooked deeper and deeper into you. So be careful.

The Quality of Your Flesh

The flesh has its hold on man, as do the world and the devil. These three important issues should be noted in sequence. The natural things *of the world war* against the spirit. Most of the worldly things we wish for stem from the *flesh or soul*. These are the things people talk about, the things we see in films or read about in books. In many ways, these seemingly harmless things have been programmed to neutralize Christians. Satan has perverted them and used them to trap people. If these things have been given priority in our lives, we are in danger. We should learn to see and judge beyond our natural realm. (See John 8:15.) Jesus pointed this out to Peter when Peter rebuked Jesus concerning His death. He admonished Peter about setting his mind on human things, as this is where his misconception of Jesus' death had originated. (See Mark 8:33.)

The devil hates it when we look at situations from God's *point* of view. He wants believers to work by sight rather than by faith. The believer who walks in the natural is no match for satan because, as long as the devil can keep the believer blind and walking in the natural, the believer is bound and *limited*. As long as Christians make decisions solely with their eyes, ears, and feelings, he has power over them.

Sin gives satan authority over us. He rules through sin. If he can keep us sinning, he has a foothold in our lives. This means that in time of temptation, we won't have the ability to fight him effectively. We are rendered weak or powerless because we have let our prayers and our quiet time go to nothing. This is even before the devil himself comes onto the scene! Most of the time, it is just our flesh *asserting* itself because of its natural propensity to sin. We ought to present ourselves unto God as living sacrifices, holy and acceptable unto Him. (See Romans 12:1-2.)

We are defeated by our flesh and desires. It is not always the devil who is in everything. We are the problem. James 1:14 says we are drawn by our desires to sin. "But each one is tempted when he is drawn away by his own desires and enticed" (NKJV).

You may just want things your own way or you may be tired of living the Christian life and want a break. Dear one, you will *break*. The Christian life *should* be a way of life!

I believe you can have your privacy, if that is what you are clamoring for, without slipping. After all, the Holy Spirit is an individual *residing* in you to guide you beside the still waters. You need not stay *away* from Him even if you stay away from Christian brethren. Staying away from the brethren can be the first step *to the edge* though, so watch it.

Kissing is another area that requires caution. Though it looks harmless, kissing is actually the *first step to full seduction*. This is the flesh, with its soulish *emotion* calling, not the devil—*yet!* Keep yourself pure. Your lips are for the Lord—a living sacrifice just as your body is. When you kiss someone on the cheek, be sure you are motivated by love to do so. This should be reserved for those who matter to you. Use it to let them know they are special. Except for this reason, it isn't prudent to go around kissing people.

Don't kiss around. If you're burning with lust, you need to get married. But wait until you are ready to marry for love, not lust. Until then, deal with your lust. Know where to draw the line. Allow the Holy Spirit living within you to help you set your standards. Don't listen to what society has to say about it. Casually kissing can deceive the other person about your intentions just as Judas Iscariot's kiss was intended to deceive. You are a holy child. Don't betray yourself and the other person with a kiss. Always behave like a child of God.

Hugging, too, is an expression of love and affection motivated from the heart. Don't give it away to just anyone. Treat it as you do your kisses. However, don't be *burdened* with the consciousness of sin. God wants you to remain the warm, caring person He created you to be! Smile, laugh, and be free. Just remember that your body *is the house* of the Holy One. He wants you to keep His house clean so that He can radiate through you to whomever you touch. Let your touch heal the sick. Let virtue flow out from you just like Jesus. Let people touch you and be made whole in their minds and bodies, rather than being ignited by lust. (See Mark 5:24-34.)

Many Christians flirt with the devil and dine with him using a long spoon. There is no need to dine with him *at all*. Why allow immoral behavior to entice you when you know it won't edify you? Why desire something just because someone else has it? When you become envious and buy something just because someone else has it, you are flirting with the devil with your money, your life, and your relationships. Pay your tithes, 10 percent of your earnings. Dedicate all you have—your possessions, money, business affairs, and loved ones—to the Lord.

The flesh and the world system became contaminated *immediately* when Adam sinned. It took only one generation for murder to creep in through Adam's son, Cain. Sin is fast and devastating. But, you are the Lord's! Look at your body as His house, not to be defiled. You must be aware of the ways touching can defile you. Kissing, as we said earlier, is not bad in itself. It is indeed a lovely exchange between husbands and wives. But if you are single, you must be sensitive when lust asserts itself and get out of the way.

You must be wise, stopping such things before they get started. All humans have a natural instinct to preserve their bodies. That is why some girls or virgins would rather die than be raped or taken advantage of sexually. Subconsciously, they are defending their *virtue*.

But when you let down your God-given hedges and allow yourself to become curious, seeking to know things you shouldn't, you allow *snakes* to come slithering in. Almost certainly you will then be bitten. At that point, you will wonder what happened! The answer is not a mystery. You broke your bond. There is a bond that holds off some experiences, and only you have the power to *break* loose those bonds. It's like the thin but strong layer of flesh that keeps and makes girls the virgins they are.

Girls, follow your instinct of self-preservation; it will never lie to you. Don't look around you or listen to anybody's advice. Don't be like a certain young prophet described in the Old Testament. God instructed him not to *drink* or *eat* until he delivered his message to the king. On his way to the king, however, this prophet met up with *another, older* prophet. The older man told the younger that he had been sent by God to invite him to dinner. The younger prophet abandoned God's direct instruction and took the word of the older prophet. Now remember, the man he encountered on the road was older, also a prophet, and said he was sent by God. Before he even continued on his way, the older prophet predicted the young man would be killed because he had disobeyed God by dining with him. On his way back home, a lion tore the prophet to bits and killed him. (See First Kings 13: 14-26.)

Don't be like the younger prophet who chose to listen to *another voice*, another instruction other than *what God told him*. Looking for other voices will always bring on disaster.

The world has its own hold on man. This is in terms of material wealth, money, fame, and power. Jesus was tempted with this as well. Luke 4:6 says: "The devil said unto Him, All this power will I give Thee, and the glory of them: for that is *delivered* unto me; and to whomsoever I will I give it." The world came under the rulership of satan when Adam sinned. In John 14:30, Jesus said, "Hereafter I will not talk much with you: for the *prince* of this world cometh, and hath nothing in me." Then Second Corinthians 4:4 states, "In whom the *god* of this world hath blinded the minds of them which believe not, lest the light of the glorious gospel of Christ, who is the image of God, should shine unto them."

These scriptures indicate that satan *rules* the earth. It is under his influence and authority. He is the god, ruler, or prince of the earth. Man was the original ruler. Genesis tells us that God gave man dominion over all things. "And God said, Let us make man in Our image, after Our likeness: and let them have *dominion* over the fish of the sea, and over the fowl of the air, and over the cattle, and over *all* the earth, and over every creeping thing that creepeth upon the earth" (Gen. 1:26).

In this life, temptation is certain to arise. You have the power to resist it, and when you do, you can sing the words to this beloved hymn: "Take the whole world but give me Jesus." The irony is that when you have Jesus, you have the whole world as well. The difference is that the world will *not* have you!

Friends can lead you astray, especially if they are materialistic. I don't think it is wise to have such people as *close* friends. They are bound to influence you, just as certainly as you will influence them. Yes, you may rub off on them, but they will rub off on you, too! Some doubts and seeds of sin will be sown in your life, the proof of which will eventually materialize. Let your confidential friends, your bosom buddies, those who you really spend time with and confide in, be serious-minded Christian believers. I don't mean those who are slack or lukewarm, but those who are truly mature. If you want to be an eagle, spend time with eagles, not chickens. As an eagle, you will soar high above all other birds and animals, far above the clouds.

The Christian life is not burdensome or tedious. It is a *meaningful* life. If you are a virgin, don't let anyone tell you that you should worry because you don't know a single thing about lovemaking. No one taught Adam and Eve. Love taught them. It is the best teacher. Being in love moves with instinct! I am sure they made the most beautiful bride and bridegroom. They produced many sons and daughters, lots and lots of children. (See Genesis 5:4–5.) Adam exclaimed in Genesis 2:23 that Eve was "bone of my bones, and flesh of my flesh." Very poetic, isn't it? No one can beat that description! They were happy and shared an active love life.

You can enjoy a happy life regardless of whether you are single, married, separated, or widowed. Enjoy the beauty of nature. Have lots of good friends and go out often. To be a child of God is to be whole and free. You have a full life ahead of you, full of sunshine with no restraint. Learn to love yourself and your singular purpose. Know all you need to know about life and be full of wisdom and knowledge. Be an example of wholeness, full of life. You can love and live wisely, the way God wants you to. You can soar like the eagle. You can be that radiance for all mankind to see, no matter your age.

4

LONELINESS

Loneliness can eat you up. Being with the Lord, however, can be a big help. As a Christian, you should not be busy dreaming up remedies for your situation. Commit your loneliness into God's hands *and let things be.*

Unfortunately, loneliness can become so intense and distracting that some singles deal with it by marrying before giving proper consideration to their decision. Many married individuals deal with loneliness by living in a dream world. Married Christians who are dealing with loneliness should work to change things. Water wears away rock with time, and the same could be true for their marriage.

If God has made promises to you, by all means stay at it, but go one step further. Instead of worrying, *chasing down every potential spouse,* or daydreaming, let the beauty of the Lord overshadow you. Throw yourself at His feet and let His mercy into your heart to chase away your loneliness. Doing this will not make you less of a person. Instead, it will give you the *relief* you seek. The love affairs, dreams, or wishes you crave will stunt and stain you. Surrendering yourself to God, even while the tortures of your loneliness still rack your being, will make you calmer, stronger, and more in control. Regardless of whether you are married or single, don't give in to the restlessness that could result in an illicit affair.

You should know that loneliness and aloneness are two *different* things. As an individual, you should enjoy the feeling of being alone. If you don't, you are already halfway *to losing your battle*. Aloneness is when you are alone *without* feeling the need for *companionship*. You enjoy your own company in a quiet place, reading, playing music, relaxing, singing, etc. You have learned to be *happy* by yourself, so much so that when someone *intrudes* on your privacy, you move to another spot. It is when you are alone that you can fellowship exclusively with the Lord, in any way or any language you like.

When you are lonely as an individual, you don't necessarily need company (plural) *but a companion* (singular). If you feel desperately lonely, direct your mind to these few words of comfort. God said, "Since you were precious in My sight, you have been honored, and I have loved you; therefore I will give men for you, and people for your life" (Isa. 43:4 NKJV). Did you get that? Another important verse is, "I will never leave you nor forsake you" (Heb. 13:5 NKJV).

His presence is near, closer to you than any person sitting nearby. He is *touchable because He is tangible!* In fact, He's living inside you, so He should be more *real* to you than anyone in the room! What you see with your two eyes is *not* as real as the Eternal. Loneliness sometimes comes with age, as you mature. So be careful what you listen to, talk about, dream, or wish for. As a Christian, you ought to feed on the right things, not lustful books, vain films, or daydreams. Feed on God's Word and godly literature as often as you can to counteract the distractions and temptations around you. Read and dwell on things that will help edify and assure you, not things that will make you seek or lust for an unnecessary mate.

If you are unmarried, listen to what First Timothy 4:12 has to say: "Let no man despise thy youth; but be thou an example of the believers, in word, in conversation, in charity, in spirit, in faith, in purity." Paul was talking to a young, single man named Timothy, who loved the Lord. Timothy was in the same situation you are in. Therefore, these words apply also to you. You are to be an example to the believers, the unbelievers, the married, and the unmarried. You are to be respected for your conduct, conversation, and your charity or love. I thank God for the example Timothy set. The Bible doesn't tell us if Timothy was dealing with loneliness, but these comforting words still apply to young men and women of every age, gender, and race.

The worst thing to do when you are lonely is to run away from it. Loneliness must be treated or it will get worse. It hinders God from using you completely, because it becomes a *need* in you. That is why you should treat it as a Christian should. You could learn to enjoy it by channeling it into aloneness. You could seek other Christian company (plural), but not just one special sister or brother. You don't need to be so afraid of loneliness that you want to run and hide. Rather say, "Yeah, I feel lonely, so what? I am human." Look it squarely in the eye. Trace it to its source. Find out the reason or occasions when you feel lonely. The best way to avoid the pain of loneliness can be found in the Book of Proverbs: *"Keep your heart with all diligence, for out of it spring the issues of life"* (Prov. 4:23 NKJV). Watch your thought life and control your desires.

Loneliness flows from the heart. You are longing for more than a companion. You are seeking someone who shares your views, ideas, values, and dreams. That is why animals could not be found to be the proper companion for man. They make good companions, but they do not share our interests and values. Eve was created from Adam's rib, specifically to be his companion. Not everyone can satisfy your heart. That's why it's important to marry the right person, your heart or soul mate. *Your dream mate.*

Crying about it won't help. You will just wear yourself out. Hunting down a partner like the lion hunts down his prey will not help either. These things are futile and they tend to become habitual. Once that happens, satan has an opportunity to rope you in. It is good to guard yourself. Never regret your self-control and discipline. The most important virtue to have in this situation is patience. Why? You need patience so that you can have the best—your very own heart's desire. So why is it taking so long, you may be asking?

You must understand that the partner you have in mind is one of your own making. He or she is a reflection of all you've loved and yearned for and hoped to find. You are looking for your perfect match. But first, God wants to make you a perfect match also! You cannot be half-baked and expect to find the perfect match. Oh, if you do meet that person, it might *click for you*. But it won't *click for that other person* until you become what he or she wants. If that time comes and you are found lacking, you could miss out on everything.

Understand this, however. Even if you find the one who fulfills your "heart's desire," your image of that person may not be complete. That person may not yet be that perfect person you desire, but he or she may have the capacity to become your special person! This is why marriage has to be an interaction—sharing, learning, studying one another, and learning to live in harmony with one another. Choose a wife who conforms to the image you have in your heart. This is like the dream God stores in His own heart for the Church. (See Ephesians 4:22-24; 5:26.) The Church is not perfect, but it has the capacity to reach the unity and perfection God *desires* before Jesus comes. Your wife should be to you what the Church is to Christ. (See Ephesians 5:25-26.) You should be willing and able to die for her and give yourself wholly for her. You should be committed to spending your life nourishing her and encouraging her in the process of sanctification so that you can present her back to God without spot or wrinkle, in splendor. You are to love your wife just like Jesus (who is the Bridegroom) loves the Church! That's what the Bible says. Do you see the comparison? Christ Jesus gave Himself up totally for us, the Church. He died and poured out His soul that He might present us without blemish to God. The key is love. Women, listen: love makes the Church *obedient* to Jesus, too.

Men should note the example Jesus laid out. Mark 9:35 says, "[Jesus] sat down, and called the twelve, and saith unto them, If any man desire to be first, the same shall be last of all, and servant of all." Then Jesus gave them an example to follow by washing His disciples' feet. "[Jesus] poured water into a basin and began to wash the disciples' feet, and to wipe them with the towel with which He was girded" (John 13:5 NKJV). When Peter objected, Jesus answered: "If I do not wash you, you have no part with Me" (John 13:8 NKJV). This passage continues:

> *When He* [Jesus] *had washed their feet, taken His garments, and sat down again, He said to them, "Do you know what I have done to you? You call Me Teacher and Lord, and you say well, for so I am. If I then, your Lord and Teacher, have washed your feet, you also ought to wash one another's feet. For I have given you an example, that you should do as I have done to you"* (John 13:12-15 NKJV).

When I think of all that Jesus, the Bridegroom, went through for His Bride, the Church, I am amazed and grateful that He felt we were worth it all. We know it was, for we are His Bride! He is determined to make us spotless and without blemish, one with Him and the Father. It is *love* that motivated Him. Now we are encouraged to follow His example:

> *Let this mind be in you which was also in Christ Jesus, who, being in the form of God, did not consider it robbery to be equal with God, but made Himself of no reputation, taking the form of a bondservant, and coming in the likeness of men. And being found in appearance as a man, He humbled Himself and became obedient to the point of death, even the death of the cross* (Philippians 2:5-8 NKJV).

Now, let us look at the wives. Just as each man has an image in his heart of what he desires his wife to be, so do most women have an image of what they desire their husband to be. Most men don't know this. You want a husband who will satisfy you, just as the Church is satisfied in the presence of the Lord. The Church is satisfied because her image of Christ has been *reached*. It tallies with her desires. It is *not* lower. No sensible woman would agree to marry a man who does not meet up to the image in her heart, her expectations.

It's unfortunate that many times in marriage, both husband and wife stop trying to conform to each other's heart's desire, and often they blame each other for this. Both become selfish and demanding. Husbands, you should know that no woman shown much love and devotion will refuse to bow to the wishes of her husband and call him lord, just like Abraham's wife, Sarah, did. Women revolt against "bossing," but love *beckons* to them. Just as love beckons the Church to Christ, your love will make it possible for her to follow your lead.

Yes, men! Women do have an image in their hearts, and if you don't measure up, she will not be satisfied and content. You cannot then expect your wife to be obedient and submissive if you are not measuring up to her heart's desires. Don't expect your wife to conform to the image of what you want in a wife if you are not trying to be the image of the husband she holds in her heart. This is a two-way street.

And women, remember that in submission all requirements are met. It is when we subject and submit ourselves to the Lord that He *gives* us our hearts' desires. Isn't it?

When one is under a higher authority, it infers *protection* as well. You, as the woman, are truly protected and covered. Someone *answers* for you and is committed to doing whatever is necessary to cover you. Just like Jesus! God says He gives men in exchange for our lives because He loves us. (See Isaiah 43:4.) So women, rejoice. There is *gain* in submission. There is joy in submission. It is a precious gift that women give to their husbands. And their husbands are charged with the responsibility to treasure it, guard it, and keep it.

When a wife rebels against her husband, there is anarchy in the family. By nagging, grumbling, and disobeying, the wife is railing against a hierarchy laid down by God. The primary characteristic of this hierarchy, however, is not dominion but love. The Holy Spirit was sent by Jesus to be a helper. Wives, you are *like* the Holy Spirit in this simple way. You were sent to be a helper to your husbands. God said Eve was created to be a helper suitable for Adam's needs. (See Genesis 1:18.) The wife stays with her husband until they are parted in death, just as the Holy Spirit abides with us until the close of the age. The work of a wife in the life of her husband should be similar to the work of the Holy Spirit in the lives of believers. Wives, that is the work you have been called to do. You are to be a helper to your husband, your children, your friends, and all those who are hurting. God has placed this deep within your nature. Resist the urge to grumble and whine, and embrace what God has created you to do.

The Bible has strong instruction for husbands as well. We read that a man who does not take care of his family is worse than an unbeliever or infidel. (See First Timothy 5:8.) Those husbands who mistreat their wives are told their prayers won't be answered. (See First Peter 3:7.) Can you see the heart of God for women?

You need not fear submission. God says that it is meet and right to submit to your husbands. You should do so in love, just as the Holy Spirit submits to God, the Father. Isn't He to be our example?

Husbands, you should be sensitive to your wives. Listen to them with your hearts. Defend and protect them. And forgive them as quickly and completely as God forgives. Forgive and forget.

The Holy Spirit submits to the Father in love and carries out the Father's will. Even Jesus submitted to the will of the Father and died on the cross for us. And what did God do? He lifted Jesus above all authority and power and placed Him at His right hand. Submission *brings* strength, character, and honor. If your husband doesn't lift you, God will. It's a law of God's Kingdom, so don't worry.

Singles, can you see that all this molding and shaping takes time? If you want to meet your dream mate, be patient. Allow God to arrange a meeting or conjunction point and *shape* each of you into the other's heart's desire. If satan can arrange a counterfeit of all you've ever wanted, then God can arrange the *genuine* article for you! The more time you waste in not succumbing to God, the longer it will take and, of course, the more *frustrated* you'll get. Remember that He wants the best for you.

See that you don't cross over to the enemy camp without knowing due to impatience and haste. Be determined not to settle for a second- or third-rate partner. You will probably be strong at first, but your intuition and knowledge will begin to wane as emotion builds up and clouds your vision. There is nothing as unsettling as emotion. It will rob you of your commitment.

Afterward, you will realize that it's too late to get the best. You are hooked! Your Christian life may suffer because one partner is much lower on the ladder than the other. However, God steps in. He loves you, remember? He cannot help but step into the situation. You are, after all, His responsibility! What God would do, in most cases, is to challenge both of you to reach a satisfactory level so that you can at least flow naturally and spiritually. Man is basically a spiritual being, so everything will fall back to this eventually. God has determined not to cross our wills, no matter how much He might wish to do so. In the end, your haste and impatience have brought you to this place. It will take time for both of you to submit yourselves to God, to build yourselves up, and to put things right. What could and should have been done before marriage now must be done within the marriage walls and the circumstances in which you find yourselves.

God understands your needs so much more than you know. Your hurt is His hurt, your sorrow His sorrow, and your joy His joy. He understands and loves the person you are, and He doesn't want anyone to *tamper* with that. He doesn't want you hurt and *trampled* upon. Don't give in to anyone who does not appreciate the special person you are. (See Matthew 7:6.) Be patient and let God fill you with His love and protect you. Open up to Him. His love, along with His grace and peace, are there for you. Ask Him to overshadow you with His love and presence as He did Mary. (See Luke 1:35.) His love will flood your soul and keep you at peace. (See Second Thessalonians 3:16.)

Another important factor to consider before you go into marriage is a calling to ministerial work. This consists primarily of pastoring, evangelism, missionary work, and the like. God does not want anything to upset His ultimate plan and calling on your life. If you are unsure about God's calling, you should first sort this out before stepping into marriage. Proper consideration on this issue can make or break you.

It is so important to know your calling so that you won't be tossed about like the waves, never able to settle on anything. Such a situation can continue for years if you are not careful. You can waste a lot of time grasping at straws. God understands! He feels what you feel, the wasted years and the frustration. He wants you to be *still*. Be still long enough for God to speak to your heart. His grace is sufficient. Be constant in Him.

Nothing can satisfy you except the will of God. Not even the marriage partner you seek. Money, career, position, and fame cannot. You will only end up searching for more, for something special. It is God you seek. There are some Christians who have grown tired of sticking to the "narrow road." Is that you? Have you been sticking there all your life, and so many times you have come close to reaching that apex God wants. But somehow you have come tumbling down each time. Now you are tired. One thing you have to know is this: it pays to be good. It gets you out of trouble! This is true for both men and women. It does pay to be good! Don't mind the caption that says, "God is busy, what can I do for you?" by satan. He will rope you into evil if you listen to him. His words might sound exciting, but they are always destructive. Eventually you, and those around you, will reap what you sow. Remember, God is faithful. Don't ever lose faith. Don't believe satan's lie. Climb right up to where you lost it and take up your stand once more.

Abraham believed God for more than twenty-five years for a son. And in those last years, it became more difficult to believe because not only was he getting older, his wife was getting older as well! She was well past the age for bearing children. But God did what He said He would do. Abraham and Sarah had a son. Then, imagine this. God asked him to sacrifice this precious boy! How on earth was Abraham going to be a father of nations through his son Isaac if Isaac died? Abraham believed God in the face of death!

Believe and trust God like a baby. Take each day as it comes with hope and gladness of heart. God is merciful and gracious. He is your heavenly Father. Have a pure heart toward Him. Do what He wants you to do and be where He wants you to be. He will definitely direct your paths and arrange things for you. He has sworn by His name. Have you ever thanked Him, truly believing that He has granted your request no matter what? Thank God with a believing heart, never doubting. Begin today with a smile!

Remember Daniel? He asked God for something, but satan, the prince of Persia, delayed his answer for twenty-one days. (See Daniel 9:20-23.) But God *did* answer and eventually Daniel got the *evidence* of his answer. He didn't give up. I believe every request you make to God is heard and answered. So rejoice, God hears the requests you make of Him. He is not deaf, so receive what is yours, and may your eyes be opened to the treasure(s) right before you. Let your heart and mind be enlightened. You asked Him, and it will come to pass!

Loneliness is for a period of time. It is a phase. It afflicts the married, the single, and God. A married person can be lonely if the other person in the marriage travels a lot or a break in communication occurs. God has a bit of it, too! He created man for fellowship, but a break in communication occurred when man sinned. Since then, He has sought to bring us back to Himself. He understands the need for fellowship, oneness, and the union of minds. Listen, God is in the business of warming hearts. He created Eve for Adam, didn't He? And for you singles? He will warm your heart with His love. We are made for the sole purpose of fellowship with God, the Father. That means you *can* be *satisfied* with Him. Be not afraid. He *will* meet your needs.

Let's look at loneliness as a "gap" rather than a disease or affliction. Gaps need filling. Loneliness is not the monster most people think it is. In fact, it can be whatever you *make* it. It can be a problem for you or a tool you can use for understanding and wisdom. Loneliness can be broken into two parts:

- A lack of human contact
- A lack of companionship

Being solely with God may not seem like enough to satisfy you because you are human with a mortal body and needs. You may feel a need to identify with *someone* human. This is normal. But ask yourself how often you feel like this? All the time? Sometimes or rarely? If your answer is all the time, something is wrong somewhere. If your answer is sometimes, you are normal. If your answer is rarely, you are at the best level to maximize your status or position. We will explain all these later. Let us take them individually.

All the Time

If you are lonely all the time, something is wrong in your relationship with the Lord. The efficiency of the Lord is demonstrated in two ways. First, He fills, and second, He is a spirit just as we are. He created us for *fellowship* with Him. He wants us to love Him and share things with Him. But the truth is that most Christians are not seeking an *intimate* relationship with the Lord. When their first love for the Lord wanes, many singles go looking for some human being to fill the gap in their lives. They turn their search to finding a companion, usually someone of the opposite sex! A relationship with someone of the opposite sex is guaranteed to give a thrill that lures the heart away from the need to get God's presence back into their lives. But seeking satisfaction and love from someone else as a substitute for intimacy with the Lord will cause a person to quickly fall into trouble. You need to identify what you are seeking and why. If you are *intimately inclined* to God, you will not *always* feel lonely. Learn to go to His innermost court and stay there. He will meet your need for companionship in His innermost court—His presence.

Sometimes

If you feel lonely sometimes, there is no need for alarm. What you have to do first and foremost is *relax*. There is no need for fear or panic. God will take control once you place it in His hands! Once you do, get busy renewing your mind. Involve yourself with constructive things and start investing in God's business, His Kingdom. Don't grab onto loneliness when it passes by. Sometimes it tries to creep in when there are fluctuations in your Christian life. Today you backslide; tomorrow you are on top. These fluctuations are not good. You should be rooted and grounded in Him.

It is possible to enjoy the feeling of loneliness, allow it to wash over you without leaving scars. In the *midst* of it, talk to the Lord. Don't *ignore* Him! It is then that you need to be in His presence *more than ever.* Don't leave Him out of it. He wants to be with you in *every* situation. When you do this, you will find that loneliness is a white-haired man illustrating wisdom. The intense and momentary depression you experience through a time of loneliness can be productively utilized to rearrange your priorities. It can be used positively as a period of deep introspection. It can create a new era in your life, if you allow loneliness to drive you closer to God. God would then be delighted to give you that practical sprint you need in your single life *as an overcomer as well as an achiever.* The sprint of *zeal and resolution* will be your *strong foothold.*

If you stay mute and seek to *cure* yourself, you may end up making things worse. The weapon satan has used on Christian believers more often than not is *relationship.* Dangerous relationships can spring from loneliness, so be careful! Don't go into a relationship foolishly. When you feel lonely, talk to God. Let it be the first thing you do. Have you done so? Do so now.

If you must seek out a companion, find a *safe* one when your emotions are not soaring high. Learn to keep a rein on those emotions. How can you know what company is safe? The best I can suggest is that you keep Christian company. If you already have a soft spot for someone and you can't restrain yourself, spend time with that person in the company of *other* people. Don't make the mistake of trusting yourself to be alone with that person. This is a difficult practice to apply. You will be stronger if you have *long practiced* the habit of being alone with God. You *will* survive; remember that! Be wise *and* cautious. It pays.

Rarely

If you rarely feel lonely, you are well on your way to maximizing your status for the work of God. You are actively involved and absorbed by His work. It is *all-consuming* to you. Your zeal for the Lord has overtaken you. Your thoughts are functioning within your love and devotion for Him. Now don't let it worry you. It's a good sign! Make use of it while it lasts. Remember loneliness will hamper you, and we don't want that!

A Need for Human Contact

The need for human contact can be for communication, companionship, or advice. You may feel that just talking with God is not quite enough. You want "physical contact" with someone. This is normal because you are not only spirit but also human. However, regardless of whether you are single or married, this can lead to trouble. It is essential that you walk *within* the principles God has laid down in the Bible. God does identify with you as a physical being. That's why He sent the Holy Spirit to live within you. He understands these feelings. Knowing this should ease the worry for you! His presence can be felt "humanly." He gave you the ability to feel. *Feelings register* to the senses. So He expects you to *feel* His presence, for He is *truly with* you. He says, "I will never leave you nor forsake you" (Heb. 13:5 NKJV).

The problem is that most people shut out their *soul's sensitivity* and their feeling of God's presence and go all *faithy*! God said we should love Him with our strength. Strength is a physical attribute! In fact, He commands us to love Him with our strength, our hearts, and our *minds.* (See Matthew 22:37.) He is actually standing with us, sitting by us, holding us. Be Christ-conscious all the time. He is a reality. Until the day we stop breathing and beyond, He will be with us.

Your need for human contact should not *cripple* you. God is your provision. He made it possible for you to survive. Therefore don't be sorrowful. Make the best possible life as you are. For as long as you *remain* in your condition, regardless of your marital status, this can be beautiful. Talk to God about *all* your desires and needs. He is capable of meeting each and every one of them in His own way and in His own time.

A Need for a Companion

This goes hand in hand with the need for human contact. In companionship, you *share* the heart desires and views of a *desirous* someone. Remember, a need for companionship is not the same as a need for company. The word *companion* is singular. It refers to a particular person that will understand and share with you. The word *company* refers to one or many. It is not as specific as companionship.

Jesus can be your *companion*, dear Christian! Remember what He said in John 15:15, "No longer do I call you servants…but I have called you friends" (NKJV). You are *My friends,* He declares! Abraham was God's great friend. They *confided* in each other. When God was on His way to destroy Sodom and Gomorrah, He told Abraham. (See Genesis 18:17.) What companionship! So great was their understanding, respect, and love for each other that Abraham was willing to sacrifice his only son to his great friend when asked to. And what a request that was! They found great favor in each other's eyes. It was a two-way street.

Consider also the great companionship between Moses and God. God had to come and show Himself physically to Moses. He allowed Moses to see His back. (See Exodus 33:15-23.)

What about David? His heart panted after God like a deer pants for water! Nothing could satisfy this men, except the Lord. David was God's friend, panting after God's desire. (See Acts 13:22.) In fact, David said he would not give to God what did not *cost* him anything.

Let's look at the apostle Paul. He gave his entire life for God. How about you? Have you given your heart, your ambition, and your desires to God? You might say that most of these men were married while you are single. But that isn't the case. Paul was single. The point is that you *may be* able to achieve so much more because you are single. If you can't do much for God now while you are unattached and free, how will you manage to achieve much when married? You have to start where you are now!

Let's look at Timothy, who was also an unmarried believer. He was *single* when Paul told him to be an *example* to all the Christian believers, in word, character, and purity. Imagine! A single unattached youth being called to be an example to *all* Christian believers of all ages and stature! Paul admonished others not to despise Timothy's youth. Now, how is that? Being young is not an excuse for laxity in Christ. People of all ages can be fruitful for the Kingdom. Young people have a large part of God's heart. (See First Timothy 4:12.) We've got lots to do!

Most scholars believe Paul never married. This shows that both conditions are good. *Look unto God!* Remember companionship is empty without an understanding or rapport between two parties. Without sharing, loneliness can afflict the married, or anyone for that matter, even in the midst of a crowd. It's true that a person might be more susceptible to loneliness if he or she is single. The good side to this is that people who have experienced loneliness are more understanding and wiser than those who have not. Let loneliness be a tool for you to use productively. Let it teach you a few things about life, human weariness, limitations, and dependence on God. Don't let loneliness cripple you. You can handle it. Don't panic.

5
THE MYTH

Let us look at the myth of the reported *sin* in the Garden of Eden. We need to do so because many single adults think it was a *sexual* sin. Some *may* want to remain single or become nuns or monks largely because of this misconception that sex is sinful. So what was the sin (known as the original sin) that took place in the Garden of Eden? Please note that *original sin* did not come from the Garden of Eden; it came from lucifer. All this will be treated in this chapter.

We will begin by taking a look at the concept of *union*. We verified earlier that God is a God of *union*. He is the originator of a union of which we are part because we are a *love* creation *from* God (we belong to Him) and *from* man (we are born due to mating). God, out of His heart, created us for fellowship, and when Jesus came to earth, He said that if we loved God and obeyed Him, He would come in *with* the Father and abide *in* us and make His home in us. (See John 14:23.) This is union. His *home* is a union with us!

In John 17:22-23, Jesus prayed to God the Father, asking that His disciples might be *one*, even as He and the Father are one. What is this? *Unity*. We have already learned that we, the Church, are the

Bride of Jesus, and He is the Bridegroom. People who love each other tend to talk a lot about each other. When you see the Bride, you've seen the Bridegroom. There are no secrets between the two. They are one. Jesus spoke of the Father all the time. He said if you have seen the Son, you have seen God the Father. (See John 14:9.) There are no secrets between them. They are one. They are in union.

Coming back to Creation, Eve was created for *union* with Adam in every way. Adam and Eve were given sexual organs *because* they were *physical* beings as well as *spiritual* beings. Now in Genesis 1:27, God created man and woman. In verse 28, He said to them, "Be fruitful, and *multiply,* and fill the earth, and subdue it." This act of multiplying *entailed* having children, and that meant having *sex*. God gave Adam and Eve a commission to have *sex before* they ate the fruit. He *gave* them sexual organs to be *used* to *mate,* have children, multiply, and fill the earth as God had instructed.

Sex was definitely intended by God in this sense because Eve was created *for* Adam. To multiply and fill the earth was His command to both of them. Adam and Eve had to *unite* not only in their *minds* but also with the *bodies* God created for them. They were physical beings. Adam rightly stated, "At last, this is bone of my bone, flesh of my flesh." This was *before* the account of sin in chapter 3.

God intended sex as the union of minds and mating. It was to be the *means* by which life is reproduced. God's purpose in the creation of sexual intimacy was not only for use in expressing a deep and physical love for one another but also for procreation. Procreation is seen immediately afterward in the birth of Adam and Eve's children. Their son Cain was born, according to Eve, *with the help of the Lord.* The birthing process was God's intention. If it were a sin and God was angry, God would not have stepped in and approved this birth by helping Eve. Genesis 4:1 says: "Adam knew Eve his wife; and she conceived, and bare Cain, and said, I have gotten a man from the Lord."

Knew, in this context, means "slept with; had sexual intercourse." It was *Adam* who slept with Eve, and the phrase "with the help of the Lord" means *definitely* that satan had *no hand* in Cain's conception. It's true that Cain later succumbed to the *voice* of satan, but not before being warned by God. He told Cain, "Sin is crouching at the door; it desires to have you, but you must master it" (Gen. 4:7 NIV). Cain decided *not* to master it. He knew the difference between good and evil, but he *chose* to do evil. He had the ability to master evil, but he *chose* not to. He was warned by God, but he didn't listen. In the next verse, we see that Cain decided to kill his own brother Abel. God wants people to choose Him *willingly*, to *listen* and *obey* without being forced. He is just like a lover. The sly one who entices and deceives is lucifer.

The Sin in the Garden of Eden

The Bible states that the *knowledge of good and evil* came when Adam and Eve ate the fruit of the tree of the *knowledge of good and evil*. We may not know exactly what that looked like, but we definitely know from the Scriptures what *it was not*. I wonder why people assume that it was something other than what God said in Genesis 3:22: "Behold, the man is become as one of us, to know good and evil." It's obvious that this happened when Adam ate from the tree rather than when he mated with his wife! If it were the other way around, it would literally mean that God had *physical* sex, that God had a wife and slept with her. God? Ask yourself, would God *do* so to be able to *know* good and evil? Of course not!

God had instructed Adam and Even not to touch the fruit of that particular tree, and it is their *disobedience* to God's clear instruction that brought sin into their world. Adam chose to listen to the *voice* of his wife rather than *obey* God. What difference does it make what was the actual fruit of the tree? The point is that it contained knowledge of good and evil, and God had forbidden them to touch it.

In Genesis 3:22-23, we read, "Now, lest he put forth his hand, and take also of the tree of life, and eat and live forever, therefore the Lord God sent him forth from the garden of Eden." This tells us two things. First of all, we learn that the fruit of the Tree of Life contains the virtue of eternal life, and second, that Adam and Eve were sent out of the garden for their own protection. God knew that if the two stayed in the garden, they might also eat of the fruit of the Tree of Life. They would then live forever in their rebellious, sinful state. Therefore, He sent them out of the garden to prevent the possibility of further harm.

The *tree of life* contained a *type of life* definitely. If a mango tree contains some ingredient that *gives* some minerals to the body, why dispute what the trees in the garden planted *by* God could give? An unripe fruit *causes* discomfort to the stomach, and some fruits can definitely *kill* when eaten! Some herbs *heal*. Why then do we doubt the trees in the Garden of Eden, a garden God planted Himself and Adam was tending?

The location of the Garden of Eden cannot be found, but a certain Tree of Life is mentioned in Revelation 2:7. Here it is said to be in the paradise of God—another location. We are told that the person who is *qualified* to eat of this tree is "him who conquers." By the way, the words *heaven, paradise,* and *Kingdom of God* do not mean the same thing. But they all definitely refer to the place where the *presence* of God overshadows. The Tree of Life is seen in Revelation 22:2 and is described thus: "On either side of the river, was there the tree of life, which bare twelve manner of fruits, and yielded her fruit every month: and the leaves of the tree were for the healing of the nations." Other references are made to stones of fire, highest throne, sides of the North, highest heaven, cherubim with wings, and more. (See Ezekiel 28:14.) There are actually stones of fire and a highest throne by the sides of the North. Ask yourself why these are not thought to mean anything else, and yet some are questioning the descriptions of the trees in the Garden of Eden.

I do believe that it was necessary to send Adam and Eve out from the Garden of Eden. They might have eaten from the Tree of Life first! Ever thought of that? When satan came into the garden, he led Eve straight to the particular tree God said they were *not to eat of*!

Let us look at what God said in Genesis 2:16-17: "You may freely eat the fruit of every tree in the garden—except the tree of the knowledge of good and evil. If you eat its fruit, you are sure to die" (NLT). Death was the result of eating from this tree. Something died inside the two of them. Though their bodies lived on, their spirits died. At one time, Adam had visited with God in the cool of the day, but that was no longer possible. (See Genesis 3:8.) Mankind began the process of sacrifice in order to seek God's face.

Physically, too, Adam and Eve began to age and deteriorate! God told them, "Unto dust shalt thou return" (Gen. 3:19). With Adam's *knowledge* of good and evil came *guilt*. He *knew* he had disobeyed God! He paid a very costly price for the knowledge of good and evil! Guilt made him feel extremely exposed. He and Eve attempted to cover themselves with leaves.

When we sin, we feel vulnerable. It is like the feeling of being naked. Until this time, Adam and Eve had been clothed in the glory of the Lord. Clothing in terms of physical *material* was not needed. But when Adam and Eve disobeyed God and ate the fruit of the forbidden tree, God's glory departed from them. They lost their "clothing." This is the same feeling we feel when the anointing or the fullness of the Holy Spirit leaves our lives. We feel empty and vulnerable. We need the covering back.

You may have sinned by lying, killing, having an abortion, or something else, and now you want to hide from God. Jonah felt the same way. He was disobedient to the voice of God to go and preach to the city of Nineveh. So he ran away and *hid* in the inner part of the ship. (See Jonah 1:1-4.)

When *God* talked about a whole church being *naked,* He didn't mean they had *no* clothes. In Revelation 3:14-17, he says:

> *I know your works, that you are neither cold nor hot. I could wish that you were cold or hot. So then, because you are luke-warm, and neither cold nor hot, I will vomit you out of My mouth. Because you say, "I am rich, have become wealthy, and have need of nothing"—and do not know that you are wretched, miserable, poor, blind, and naked* (NKJV).

They were *naked* because the glory of God had departed from the church at Laodicea. God asked them to buy white garments from Him to clothe themselves and keep the shame of their naked-ness from being seen. (See Revelation 3:18.) Married couples glory in the nakedness of each other's bodies. Why would this be if it is sin? When Adam saw Eve for the first time, she was naked, and he reveled in her beauty, so much so that he exclaimed, "At last, flesh of my flesh."

But the nakedness that comes from *disobedience* to God leaves us naked *literally.* Adam, because he was sensitive to God, felt his phys-ical nakedness when the glory of God departed, since that glory was their covering in every sense. He felt exposed, so he found leaves to cover their nakedness.

Now apart from disobedience, satan was sly in his advice to Eve to eat fruit from the forbidden tree. He had his reasons. He not only wanted man to *disobey* God but also to become subject to death, which was the end result of disobeying by eating the fruit of the forbidden tree. He wanted death to become part of man's *nature.* He introduced the *concept* of sin as well as the spe-cific sin itself. Sin brought in all manner of *distortion*: death in ex-change for life, lust for love, lies for truth, sorrow for joy, pain for pleasure, and the list goes on. This was a smart move on satan's part. If he could entice the woman with a suggestion, he would gain access to God's whole creation. (See Genesis 3:5.)

No one teaches a baby to tell lies or do wrong. The sin nature was passed down from Adam and Eve through this bloodline and has contaminated the whole of mankind, as we are all their descendants. In the blood is life. (See Genesis 9:4.) Doctors would tell you so. Because sin was embedded in the blood, only a blood sacrifice could atone for it. This is why God instructed His people to sacrifice animals—rams and sheep, for example—to cover their past sins. To overcome the sin nature once and for all, though, a *spotless* blood had to be shed, the blood of Jesus, called the Lamb of God. He *bought* us over so that He could bring the Holy Spirit into our lives to *infuse* a new birth into our beings. (See Hebrews 9:12-14.)

Lucifer was an angel before sin was *found* in him. Sin came in the form of pride in his beauty and achievements. He was the most beautiful angel created, and he desired to be seen and worshiped as God. He was not *tempted* or *lured*. Lucifer, now known as satan, was kicked out of heaven with the rest of the angels he wooed and contaminated. We read lucifer's story in Ezekiel 28:11-19. He can take the form of an *angel* anytime. Evil spirits need physical bodies. In Mark 5:9-13, we read that a "legion" of evil spirits had possessed a man and driven him mad. When Jesus cast the demons out, they begged to be cast into a herd of pigs *rather than* be cast away.

Lucifer had set himself to fight against God and contaminate *everything* created in heaven and earth, everything in the *vast* universe. He wished to pollute the whole of creation itself. Anything within his reach was targeted, the spiritual, the physical, and everything in between! His goal is to permeate everything with his distorted nature. He has a raging anger against all that God created and loves. And that definitely includes *us*. Let's determine not to be deceived by his coercive and sly ways. The end product, what he has set out to achieve in any manner, is to subtly but surely turn us away from God and *against* God. But we thank God who knows all things. Victory is His—and ours—through the *sacrifice* of

Jesus. (See Revelation 20 and 21.) May our eyes be open to the revelation that was predestined by God Himself.

Turning again to the origin of sin *on earth* in the Garden of Eden, I believe that *disobedience is making the* wrong *choice* of whom to *believe* and *obey*. If it was actually a sexual sin at issue, God had another chance to change His instruction to mankind shortly after the flood. Instead, God chose to save Noah and his family during the flood and said to them afterward:

> *Be fruitful and multiply, and fill the earth. And the fear of you and the dread of you shall be upon every beast of the earth, and every bird of the air, on all that move on the earth, and on all the fish of the sea. They are given into your hand. Every moving thing that lives shall be food for you. I have given you all things, even as the green herbs* (Genesis 9:1-3 NKJV).

"Multiply" means *having sex for procreation*. God told Noah and his sons the same thing He told Adam and Eve. This time they were *not* in the Garden of Eden and *the tree was not there!* Sex was intended by God as an expression of love, a union of mind and body to produce life and birth. It is beautiful to know that we are all products of multiplication through sex. All the different races in this whole, wide universe are part of that instruction from God. (See Genesis 1:27.)

God wants us to enjoy life absolutely, to the core. That is why He made us the way He did and created our sexual organs for maximum sensual satisfaction. We didn't ask for it. We were created!

And God didn't create us to cheat us—that is lucifer's lie, his insinuation. He made this simple insinuation by stating the commandment given to Eve as a *question*. "Did God say you shouldn't eat of any tree from the garden?" This question—made as an insinuation—makes it appear that God is withholding from us. Lucifer knew what the commandment was before he went to Eve. He used the *exact command* given to them—not to verify, but to *insinuate*. It was as simple as that! By this insinuation, lucifer wished to place doubt in Eve's mind, the same doubt he placed in the hearts and minds of the angels in heaven when he caused them to rebel. He started the *rebellion* against God's authority *and* integrity. By this, the angels corrupted themselves. This corruption was a *direct* rebellion against the authority of the *governorship or lordship* of God. Lucifer coaxed Eve in the same way. Eve's choice was not a direct rebellion to the lordship of our sovereign God but a disobedience to a *given* command *not to eat from a tree*. (Note that sin was in existence already; it *had emerged* and started in lucifer, its father.) In Eve's mind there was no thought of dethroning God's lordship over her life as with the offending angels. Our Lord God, to her mind, still remained her God and Master. She had little understanding of satan's ploy. Let us look closer to what I call the challenge.

The Challenge

God had made angels in a nonphysical realm in a first creation, and they inhabited heaven. Back then lucifer was adorned with the most precious stones and pearls and was perfect in beauty. He was called the day star and son of dawn until sin was found in him. Lucifer was tempted by no one; sin emerged from him because he "turned" inward into himself, and this is *selfishness*. God is the opposite. God is "*outward.*" God turns around to *give, to create, to share*. God is the *manufacturer* and has written a manual for us, the Bible. Lucifer decided to use a different manual and wrought in himself dissatisfaction and turmoil. The outcome was the opposite of what God intended. He *malfunctioned*. He then became the father of sin and evil. Covetousness, lying, stealing, murder, and all other sin erupted. *It became a chain, multiplying, and perpetuating itself.*

We can thank and praise God that He is good and the source of all things good. He is the s*ource* of our existence and all the goodness in our lives. This in *itself* is a *salvation* from sin. In the beginning, God made all things good, and our salvation comes from that goodness. Sin came *afterward*. Satan came afterward. God is the only one who can know good *and* the capacity of evil and *remain untarnished* because darkness or sin *cannot abide* in Him. He is the All-Knowing and so *knows*. That is why His Word says we are to *"overcome evil with good."* (See Romans 12:21.) Conquer evil by doing good. What can overcome evil is good, any time, any day. It may be a matter of time, but this is what is designed to overcome evil in its nature. Strike a match in pitch darkness, and you will see how the darkness fades away! No matter how dark, just strike a match! We do not have to fear darkness because we are by *relationship with* the light. Read Romans 12:20-21 and understand this properly.

Hallelujah, our Creator is *all knowing and all good*! Good always overcomes evil ultimately, and it always will.

Note that for lucifer to oppose God, he had to have freedom of choice. This tells you that God is fair and does not compel His angels to worship Him. They worship Him because they desire to do so. They are filled with His love and stand in awe of Him. They see His holiness constantly, for they abide within its atmosphere. Do you know what holiness means? Holiness is *pure goodness, pure love, and pure all that is good and fair*. Who could stand before that and fail to bow in worship? Who would *not* succumb to *love* so great? That lucifer did *oppose God* shows that he had freedom of choice, *and more so,* it shows *the extent* of his inward shifting. He was preoccupied with the assumption of his own self-importance.

God does not create any thing or being without freedom of choice. In Genesis 6:1-2, we read, "When people began to multiply on the face of the ground, and daughters were born to them, the sons of God saw that they were fair; and they took wives for themselves of all that they chose" (NRSV). There's a choosing here.

It continues in verse 4 of the same chapter: "The Nephilim were on the earth in those days—and also afterward—when the sons of God went in to the daughters of humans, who bore children to them" (NRSV). Because the passage distinguishes between the "sons of God" and the "daughters of humans," we understand that they were of a different species. The sons of God were angels. The angels chose wives and produced children, giants known as Nephilim. They are mentioned in Numbers 13:33, when Moses sent spies into Canaan who reported that they had been as grasshoppers compared to those who lived in the area.

The angels who rebelled were not forced to disobey. God allowed them the freedom to choose as He does with all His creation. That's His nature. Even the serpent was coaxed by lucifer. We read that the serpent was craftier than all the wild animals the Lord had created. Its punishment for this was to crawl on its belly from then on. (See Genesis 3:1,14.)

Lucifer's opposition was to usurp God's position—make no mistake about that. "I will ascend into heaven, I will exalt my throne above the stars of God" were his very words in Isaiah 14:13. What he was in essence telling the angels in heaven was this, "Hi guys, God is the selfish one; He doesn't want us to enjoy ourselves. All we do is worship Him and do His bidding." (He whispers the same insinuation to us today!) He continued with the angels, "Come on, we can do better! Come away with me, and let's do our own thing. This way, we will rise above the stars and the things of God, and overthrow God's sovereign authority!" A *coup d'etat* was getting ready to take place. It wasn't just that these agitating angels had a different view or mindset. No! It was *anarchy* arising. It started from satan's bosom and begat after its kind—discord, disquiet, uproar, discontentment, and the rest.

It is only when you do God's will that you can be content and fulfilled. You will turn *restless with less*. It was a lesson these fallen angels needed to learn. And yet, some angels listened! A third of them turned inward to themselves and decided to *dethrone* their Creator. *The Rebellion* was underway. God's very *nature* was in question, His goodness, integrity, and righteousness. The question that resounded throughout the creatures of the heavens was this—*is God fair?* This question, insinuated by lucifer, became a seed. God watched as the angels loyal to Him defeated lucifer and his conspirators and cast them out of heaven. Jesus said in Luke 10:18: "I saw Satan fall like lightning from heaven" (NKJV). Then God decided to do something. *He began to create the world for mortals and us humans.* This question and insinuation of fairness had to be settled once and for all.

How would it be decided? That was the purpose behind the creation of a physical world with human beings "made in the image of God but a little lower than the angels." (See Hebrews 2:7.) Jesus and the Holy Spirit knew of this and consented when God said, "Let us make man in our image." It was the *mystery* of the ages to be unraveled and unveiled. Humans would settle the score and teach the fallen angels something they needed to learn. They would freely display the righteousness of God. Good and bad were going to be played out in the universe, all gloves were off, and all created beings both visible and invisible would see what is right and true. They would know who was greater, not just by might but also by measure.

The Lamb of God opted to live and die for us. (See Hebrews 10:5-7; Revelation 5:2-10.) God gave of Himself. He emptied Himself to die on a cross and be the ransom for sin. (See Hebrews 9:26.) What would it take to ransom the *devastation* of *sin?* What would it take to eradicate those devastating effects that had been birthed in lucifer? What did it take? Everything God had to give! It boiled down to ransoming those He *loved* and making a journey that has enveloped what I call "worlds" (the world that was, the world that is, and the world to come). We were predestined—we are now and we will be. Jesus, who has been from eternity with God, had to agree to humble Himself and be born in the likeness of man, to be lashed brutally—the pain dispersing to every atom, every nerve, every fiber—and *to die*. Psalm 22:14-15 says, "I am poured out like water, and all My bones are out of joint: My heart is like wax; it is melted in the midst of My bowels. My strength is dried up like a potsherd." He cried out when it was beyond measure, "My God, My God, why hast Thou forsaken Me?" (Matt. 27:46). The lashes and pain Jesus underwent echo through eternity, now and forever.

Two questions erupted in the dispute that raged in heaven. They were: 1) Is God fair? and 2) Would any created being *voluntarily* worship God after knowing good and evil? This was now the question. Was it fair for God to punish and exile those angels who chose not to worship Him and take their place alongside lucifer? In order to rightly understand this, all aspects—the good and the bad with their consequences and results—must be displayed.

The fallen angels chose sin through opposition to God's *direct* rule. The angels on God's side, however, *knew no sin*. So how was this going to be settled? Did the accusation have some glimmer of truth of God's injustice? Another disturbing factor was this: the angels were also rebelling against the authority of governorship by God. This was God's very right to be in authority over them—to be God and be worshipped as God. So by this very act, they had not only rejected God's position and authority but rejected the acceptance of His very nature and His person. This could not be swept under the rug. The challenge to God's authority had to be met and dealt with. God cannot leave any seed not birthed by Him to germinate and grow. It would germinate, grow, and multiply after its kind—sin. Then it would do its devastating work.

As God began His creation, the angels watched and wondered, and lucifer raged. We, the beloved ones, were now predestined. (See Ephesians 1:4-5, 9-12.) The stage was set. All that was needed was His creative hand, which He set in motion with loving care. He took His time creating the world and creating us. He did so with great detail, numbering even the hairs on our heads. (See Matthew 10:30.) It is lovely to be alive and be predestined!

Oh, I know this one thing, God our Father knew that we would take the bait of "knowing good and evil." It hurt Him to know even then that an already-infected lucifer would induce Eve to disobey. He is all-*knowing*, remember? He knew the choice Adam would make, and He knew its importance and the role it would play. The tree was placed in the garden to offer Adam and Eve a *choice*. Then the choice to shut God out was placed there as well when God told them not to touch the fruit of the Tree of the Knowledge of Good and Evil. Remember, He had "predestined us *before* the creation of the world in *Christ*." (See Ephesians 1:11.) And so, when God came walking in the garden during the cool of the day, His heart was burdened. He already knew what had happened, but He came seeking His beloveds anyway.

Step into the heart of love and see! This is the Lord God, our Father. How can we choose our world in exclusion of Him? How can we ever think it will work? How can we exclude His voice, His advice, His desires in our lives, in our marriages, and in our relationships? We have tried, and we can see the results.

Meanwhile in the Garden of Eden, God watched and waited. Time stood still.

If Adam and Eve had not eaten of the forbidden tree in spite of lucifer's coaxing, it would have been a shorter route to prove God's sovereign goodness, fairness, and rightness. He didn't *have* to *prove* it. He wanted to *show* it. He knew that if we caved in, He would see it through to its outcome, the end (and so would lucifer).

Lucifer started the plot to get Eve to disobey God by using a member of the cattle family now called a serpent. His plan was to get into our physical world, as this was his only connection to the seen physical world. There was no link or connection between him and

Adam and Eve anyway. They didn't know *who* he was, neither was he ever *introduced* to them. They knew no concept of sin, nor had they ever seen lucifer. They knew only that which was in the garden. All the animals interacted with them, and the serpent was known to them, so when it approached and spoke, Eve was not surprised.

But God wasn't going to allow His world and creation to be polluted—not by sin and certainly not by satan's cunning. This was, after all, His master plan, *not* lucifer's. He saw Eve cave in, but God can use all things (good and bad) to work them according to His purpose. (See Romans 8:28.)

Lucifer does not have this ability. He uses that which is within his domain to continue his reign. When Jesus came onto the scene on our planet Earth, satan welcomed the opportunity to kill Him. He immediately knew who Jesus was. When Jesus was conceived by the virgin Mary, satan attempted to kill Him through Herod, who ordered the slaughter of all male children under two years of age. But the plan failed. When Jesus was older, satan tried to tempt Him to give up His purpose. He may have been thinking, *If I can't kill Him, I'll corrupt Him. I'll fill His spirit with my seed. If I can get Him to listen to me, like Adam and Eve did, I can rule over Him and the earth will be forever under my control!* This was his plan, but he failed yet again. Thank God! Jesus' temptation in the wilderness was a cornerstone in the course for salvation.

Then lucifer screamed, "I must kill Him. I will crucify Him!" Ha! Ha! That was what Jesus came *for* after all! The works of satan would cause him to dismantle himself with his own hands. Poetic justice! God is the only *One* who can use *all things* to work according to His purposes! A marvel. A wonderful thing. The Creator watched as lucifer dug a pit with his own hands and fell in. Lucifer can no longer accuse God indirectly or otherwise. Nope! He did this himself. He carried out his plan to crucify Jesus. He recruited Judas Iscariot, convinced the high priests, orchestrated the crowd to demand His death, and killed the Son of God. God watched, knowing that the precious, spotless blood of the Messiah, His Son, would not be spilled for nothing. Because of its purity, it would save and uphold to the uttermost.

Call on the blood of Jesus anytime, anywhere, in any plane, dominion, or sphere and watch its power unfold. (See Colossians 1:15-20.) It is the blood that speaks not only in this life but in that which is to come. Lucifer, beclouded by his greed, wanted to get rid of the Son of God! For him, killing the Lamb of God meant dominion forever on the planet he came to acquire as his throne! He planned and caused his own permanent doom. What a laugh! His big blunder was revealed when Jesus walked boldly out of the grave where death ruled. Without sin and laying down his life as a sacrifice, Jesus took the keys of death. Remember God's words to Adam: *the day you shall eat of the tree, you shall die.* Death ruled all whom lucifer had captured and chained. But Jesus' victory over death made lucifer an open mockery, and his captives, both then and now, have been set free. Hallelujah!

It is no longer a battle to establish the "fairness of God" or the dominion and rulership of planet Earth that lucifer is fighting for. The ground has shifted yet again for him. In his anger and frenzy, he seeks to take as many souls as he can with him to his final place, Hades! His mind is vengeful. It is the mind of a destroyer.

Jesus came into the world to set us free by offering Himself in our place, and *He paid in full the price for sin—the obstacle* that had separated us from God, our Father, for generations as our ancestors multiplied and filled the earth.

By dying, Jesus set us free from the *sting* of sin. By rising and sitting at the right hand of God, He set us free from *death.* We can now say "death, where is thy sting?" Jesus' suffering on the cross of Calvary and the forgiveness it bought is as fresh today as it was yesterday when it was offered up and poured out. Time has not changed it.

Let us join the winning team comprised of God, the cloud of witnesses mentioned in Hebrews 12:1, and tens of thousands of holy angels! (See Revelation 5:11.) Let us give our love and life voluntarily to God. He's worth it. He proved that by giving everything He had to pay for our sin. We are His beloved humans, those who are made and created a little lower than the angels, those who have been given the wonderful choice of revealing to all of creation that, though we have experienced good and evil, we *choose good*. We choose *Him*. We choose this with our *free will*. One day soon, lucifer will be shut up literally for eternity and his accusations put to rest forever! Our God has *shown* His *exceeding* love and greatness by His involvement with man. Even while we were sinners, He loved us and came to die for us in order to redeem us from the clutches of sin and death.

We must, therefore, look beyond the works of lucifer, which are manifest in the turmoil and havoc in our world, and have no fear. We are *hidden* in the shelter of the Most High. We should not fear the terror of the night or the arrow that flies by day. We should not fear the pestilence that stalks in the darkness or the plague that destroys at midday because the Most High is our dwelling place. (See Psalm 91.) We are engraved in the palms of His hands, and He knows us by name, every single one of us. We are on the winning team! Jesus, *in the form of man,* accomplished this for us as we accept Him and His redemptive power into our lives. Now when we call on God, our Father, we already know that we are conquerors. Calling on God is to pray. Praying is talking and agreeing with Him. Prayer is simplified if we can only understand this concept. He requires this communication, this fellowship. Let us look at it briefly.

When we pray we are in agreement with God. He wants us to be in agreement with Him and to partner with Him to get things done. Remember, He didn't go ahead and create the world and man without *partnering* with the Holy Spirit and Jesus. When God wanted to create, He partnered with them. He said in Genesis 1:26, "Let *us* make man in *our* image." Genesis 1:2 says, "The Spirit of God was hovering over the surface of the waters" (NKJV). In the Book of John, we read that God created *everything* through *Jesus, the Word,* and nothing was created except through Him. Jesus, the Word, gave *life* to everything that was created. (See John 1:3.)

That is true even now. He had given Adam authority over all the earth, and though Adam foolishly gave this authority to satan, Jesus bought it back for us at the cross by His death and resurrection. Humans are spirit beings, made in His image. When we pray, God can and will legally bring it forth and give it to us. That's a legal partnership I would say! God wants to work with us. Hallelujah! Matthew 16:19 says, "I [the Lord] will give you the keys of the kingdom of heaven, and whatever you bind on earth will be bound in heaven, and whatever you loose on earth will be loosed in heaven" (NKJV).

But we see that Jesus was made *a little lower than angels* in order to suffer death for man. Then, by the grace of God, He tasted death *for everyone* and paid the price for sin *eternally*. Jesus, though man, is God and is eternal. His payment for sin, therefore, *became* eternal, as well. (See Hebrews 9:25-26.)

Philippians 2:5-8 says:

> *Let this mind be in you which was also in Christ Jesus, who, being in the form of God, did not consider it robbery to be equal with God, but made Himself of no reputation, taking the form of a bondservant, and coming in the likeness of men. And being found in appearance as a man, He humbled Himself and became obedient to the point of death, even the death of the cross* (NKJV).

Jesus came in the *form of man,* for the plan to dismantle the sinful works of satan was to be achieved through mankind. We read in Hebrews 2:14 and 16:

Because God's children are human beings—made of flesh and blood—the Son also became flesh and blood. For only as a human being could He die, and only by dying could He break the power of the devil.... We also know that the Son did not come to help angels; he came to help the descendants of Abraham, not to help the angels (NLT).

Jesus' goal was the redemption of man from sin, from lucifer's clutches. Philippians 2:9-11 says:

Therefore God also has highly exalted Him [Jesus] *and given Him the name which is above every name, that at the name of Jesus every knee should bow, of those in heaven, and of those on earth, and those under the earth, and that every tongue should confess that Jesus Christ is Lord, to the glory of God the Father* (NKJV).

The first ten chapters of the Book of Hebrews describe all this. Please read this book and mark it with a highlighter. You will see why Jesus came and what His role was. I pray that your eyes will be opened.

[God,] *having made known to us the mystery of His will, according to His good pleasure which He purposed in Himself, that in the dispensation of the fullness of the times He might gather together in one all things in Christ, both which are in heaven and which are on earth—in Him* (Ephesians 1:9-10 NKJV).

God, who is rich in mercy, because of His great love with which He loved us, even when we were dead in trespasses, made us alive together with Christ (by grace you have been saved), and raised us up together, and made us sit together in the heavenly places in Christ Jesus, that in the ages to come He might show the exceeding riches of His grace in His kindness toward us in Christ Jesus (Ephesians 2:4-7 NKJV).

Indeed it will be like the Bible says in First Corinthians 6:2-3, that *saints* shall judge the world and angels. Some selected saints, I presume. Amazing!

6

MATURITY

Maturity is not measured in clothes or the amount of smiles you flash (as if you were counting smiles). Maturity is the *substance* of the hidden man. It is how we interact with the environment around us, our reactions. Jesus is the one we follow. Through Him we have access to the throne room of grace. We were destined to be made perfect in Him. Jesus lived as a man and was tempted in all points as we are. That is why He can *identify* with our weakness and temptations. (See Hebrews 4:15; Hebrews 2:14-18.)

Temptation

Some people think Jesus wasn't tempted sexually, emotionally, or financially. In Genesis 6:2-7, we read that, at some point, angels came and married women on earth and had children that grew into giants on the earth. The Bible refers to them as "sons of God." If this is true, Jesus must have been tempted to live as a natural man should! He lived among us as a man for 33 years. He was made *flesh* after all! He could have chosen to settle down with a wife and children.

Thank God, He overcame the desire for that human need as well as satan's temptations in the wilderness after His baptism.

Thank God, He triumphed over all things, was revealed when His time came, and began His ministry. A lesser man, whose "zeal for God" had not consumed Him, might have settled for less. Jesus knew His *sole* purpose and *gunned* for it.

We have to understand that He was made a "little lower than the angels." He was made flesh. *A body* was prepared for Him. (See Hebrews 10:5.) He felt hunger, weakness, and fatigue after a long day. He slept at night. How then do you think He cannot identify with your temptations? The Bible says He was tempted in *all* points as we are. (See Hebrews 2:14-18.) I believe that! He was flesh and blood, able to cry. That was an emotion! In the same measure, He was tempted by the devil at all points of His life down to the crucifixion day!

In the Garden of Gethsemane, His sweat became as drops of blood. But He overcame all without sin or guile. That is why I said that the mystery *lies* with Jesus—the mystery to life, love, emotions, and self-control. He had the unique balance. He can intercede for us to the Father. He was one with God in mind, purpose, and maturity while living here on earth. Having *one* spirit with Christ will mature anyone! This is because Christ transfers His righteousness and maturity *into* us. He infuses His type of life inside us so that we automatically become overcomers. Maturity lies in Christ. Seek after His heart, nothing more. Job 32:7-9 says, "I thought, 'Age should speak; advanced years should teach wisdom. But it is the spirit in a man, the breath of the Almighty, that gives him understanding. It is not only the old who are wise, not only the aged who understand what is right'" (NIV).

Be Yourself!

Many believers lose their identities because they are trying to be like the crowd. They throw away their natural friendliness for a flimsy façade that doesn't suit them. They become bottled up, change their wardrobes, and shake hands rather than hug one another. They cannot jump and praise God anymore. They cannot cry because of their makeup. They are conscious of their jewelry and their appearances because they are at the forefront, always being seen.

Release yourself to be your true person. Allow the Holy Spirit to lead you in these areas, too! Sometimes the Spirit may want you to look natural, without cosmetics. He may be impressing on you to wear your hair up or down. Whatever it is, you will feel comfortable with it. Don't be hindered by mere clothing, which would have taken a little bit of "obedience" to overcome!

Another time, He may want you to feel the excitement of dressing up. You can wear your suit, jewelry, or lipstick with joy! Listen to God about what you wear, not other people. Know what you want to *portray* by and *with the Spirit*. Dressing should be your spirit man's expression. Individuality is encouraged. This calls for constant sensitivity. Don't copy others. Don't worry about the girl who wears pants, slacks, and jeans, if that doesn't fit your style. Forget about the guy who wears a suit or slacks and a blazer with a chain and earring if that doesn't appeal to you. Don't feel you have to wear what they wear. Wear what you feel like wearing, what fits you and the *mood* of the Spirit. When He changes, you change.

We have to be honest about these things with God. Many have lost their identities while copying others. Have your own style, feel the Spirit. It grieves me to see simple-hearted girls changed into monsters for the sake of fitting in with the crowd. Let the Holy Spirit shine from within! It is not childish to be smiling most of the time! People simply differ in character and nature. As tongues and gifts differ, we differ as individuals. What you are is not what everyone else should be! Learn to love each individual character, gift, and talent. God made us different, so why shouldn't you enjoy expressing your own unique personality and talents. Despite our different personalities and expressions, we are one in the Lord.

Sometimes I watch those who try so hard to copy others' clothes, hairstyles, and even their language patterns, and they simply look out of place! It just doesn't fit them. Some people—men and women—look best in simple clothing. The irony is that when people try so hard to fit in, they make themselves stand out even more. Anyone can pick them out.

There is a carefree character that reveals maturity. Some have smiling faces full of grace, others serene faces full of wisdom, still others sober faces full of character. All are in God. Let people be. And be who you are. Grow in your own way of expressing yourself. Make sure your inner man is built up, rooted, and grounded in God. Wherever you may be, whatever you are comfortable wearing, your maturity *will* show.

Maturity has a way of showing itself at the end. Some people you *think* don't have it might have it more than you think. You don't know what is in the spirit or heart of a person. This person may surprise you one day, so don't be scornful.

The type of job you've got does not always signify the level of your maturity. Some people think those who work in banks are more responsible. They think doctors or engineers are more responsible. Some judge by talents and looks. How wrong can we get? How we have missed it! We may think we are better informed than the early Christians, while instead we may be in danger of destroying once more the simplicity of the Gospel!

It is the balanced, mature person who can see through to the core of a matter and weigh it out. A mature person is tuned in to what is going on. Mature people are able to subtly transfer their abilities and character to others, not by enforcing or belittling, but by *living among* them as examples. Those around them are automatically affected. We are influenced by the good character and maturity of those we meet. Jesus had a flawless character while on earth, and that is why people were drawn to Him.

Maturity is not related to education. Having a degree does not make you mature. Some church workers in Gospel ministry feel inferior to those who hold degrees. Oh, they don't say it, but they often feel it. The interesting thing is that some educated, working people feel inferior to those in ministry! The point is that education doesn't make you mature. God has told us not to compare ourselves with others. God places us where we should be and appoints us to what we should be doing. Obeying Him should be the objective.

God distributes the gifts and talents. Don't begrudge others what is theirs. In job seeking, don't go solely for the money or status. Do what you would love and enjoy doing, even if you are not paid for it. Love your job enough to put in extra hours. Choose jobs that exercise your natural talents. Choose something you love doing, desire to do, or desire to be.

Maturity is not about size—whether you are tall, of medium height, short, or fat. It has nothing to do with your features. You may be a social butterfly or naturally shy. God can use either. You may have masculine features or be baby-faced. You may or may not have muscles. You may be slender or voluptuous. None of these things signify maturity.

Maturity is the hidden man in God. How God wants you to reach your maximum potential in your own individual way! This will give Him joy. Who could ask for more than becoming all God has created you to be.

7

PERSONAL CRISIS

Some situations leave us with a feeling of betrayal and disappointment. Those with an inferiority complex are left to feel that they may not be up to what they should be. It is important, regardless, to reclaim your self-esteem and get back on your feet. Don't let depression or self-castigation keep you from reaching your goals. Be of *strong* character, not for your family and friends, but for yourself. Ease your mind by spending time with good friends who have positive attitudes and are of good reputation. They should be people you can share with. If you don't have friends like this, look around you. Find some you admire for the right reasons and seek them out. That's the first step. Don't tolerate loneliness. Get out and make friends with people who are friendly and kindhearted. Even if your new friend or friends don't have the same problems you have, they will still be able to encourage you. If you take this step, you are on your way up. Be of good courage and be of good cheer. Always be cheerful. This is the key. Don't be weighed down. Life is for the living!

The Bible says to "Count it all joy when you fall into various trials, knowing that the testing of your faith produces patience" (James 1:2 NKJV). Deal with your thought life. Stop analyzing things, feeling you have no friends, goals, or achievements. Such thoughts will only get you down, and they are lies anyway. Turn those thoughts away. Shut them out in the cold. You can control your mind! Laugh a lot with your friends and spend plenty of time in the presence of God. Don't ever give in to negative thoughts. They are, by nature, killing thoughts!

A change of scene and job might help in some situations, but friend, make no mistake—this problem is in your *mind*. That's where it must be dealt with. You can change jobs or move to a new place, but until you deal with your negative thoughts, they will follow you from one job to the other, one place to the other. Contentment and settling down is a mind issue. Decide that the next job you take or place you go will be more fulfilling because you are going to *be* settled. *Believe that.* Only you can settle that *restlessness* in your heart. Changing places and jobs won't do it. Settle your heart now. Put your mind at rest!

As a Christian adult, you ought to be free to enjoy life! That is the beauty of being young. Even if you are older, you should let your heart go, knowing that your life has purpose. You were created for a purpose by God. But you will never find real rest until you go to Him and find out what it is. He is not far. (See Acts 17:27.) In fact, He is as close as your heartbeat. Talk to Him and don't shy away and ignore Him. The world is before you just as it always has been. You have a lot of life still ahead of you. Listen to the music, enjoy the scenery, meet new people, and make new friends.

If you have been hurt or disappointed by a friend in the past, let it go. Everyone experiences those hurts at times. They are part of life. Not everyone is bad and uncaring in a world as full and large as ours. Have you considered sports? Don't be cooped up in the house with your moody thoughts.

Don't make the mistake of thinking you will have friends if you don't go out and get them. And when these friends come, don't send them away because you aren't in the mood! The joke is on you, buster. Snap out of it! Use your mind to come up with positive ideas. Consider travel or a cruise, maybe even a picnic. There are many things for Christians to do.

Remember too, to take opportunities to talk to others about your Master. Learn to identify with Him. When asked who you are, don't hesitate to say you are a child of God. Don't hide from it. Say it! It will save you a lot of trouble if you do, and most likely would create further grounds for new friendship.

Don't let a conversation come up without identifying yourself as a child of God. If you are sensitive, you will find many opportunities to talk about the Master. There is *safety* in being on the Lord's team. God will not begrudge you your fun if you identify with Him. But you are His child, and don't be ashamed to say so! It *is the* natural thing to say! Jesus said He came to give you abundant life. (See John 10:10.) Friends worth having will be glad to hear you are a Christian. Trust God. He wouldn't hurt you. The Lord never does. He *knows* more than you. Simply identify with Him when you get the chance and live safely and happily.

Taken for Granted

Some Christians have problems with forgiveness. They feel people have taken them for granted, so much so that they can no longer forgive the person involved. You may have taken someone for granted at one time in your life. We all have. We also take *life* for granted. That's why we tend to brood about things and find it difficult to forgive. When we feel like quitting, we are taking life for granted because we feel life isn't worth living. Can't you see that?

If people take us for granted, it is because they don't know better. You should value yourself. Anyone who disregards you has lost out. Believe that and don't be intimidated or grieved! Believe you are a precious gem. Be more mature than the other person and extend your friendship into that relationship when you feel it's right to do so.

If you have been rejected by someone of the opposite sex, then it is good riddance, especially if you were considering marriage to that person. No spouse should continually take the other for granted. If you make efforts to do the right things, your spouse should not overlook or tread on them. If you are a Christian adult and you want to marry a mature, responsible, dedicated Christian, *go* where you will find such people. Attend church activities. Get involved in church programs!

If you are a strong, dedicated Christian yourself, take up an activity in the church. Be involved, because that is where you will find others like yourself! If you are "a normal Christian at home," then other normal Christians will meet you at home (where you are). Eagles don't fly with pigeons. If you are an eagle, go where the eagles fly, *in the skies above the clouds.* Don't go to where hens are pecking on the ground and expect to catch an eagle. The chances are that you will catch a hen or be a hen yourself! You might even catch a cockroach—after all, it has wings!

A Break in Communication

A loss of communication in any relationship will breed uncertainty and insecurity. First of all, if your communication with God has been broken, go back! Restore and build up that relationship. This is *most* essential. Make *the effort* to go back. However, if you have been making an effort and blowing it, stop and let God take over. God will help you get rid of that habitual sin if you will just go to Him as you are. Go back and read the section on spiritual feeding. His presence will fill your soul and spirit.

A lack of communication between friends and spouses can easily breed misunderstanding. You might go different ways without knowing. By communicating, the other person will relate to and understand you properly, hearing what you are really saying. Often in relationships, a time comes when one party takes the other for granted. You have to understand that since your partner is not you, it would be impossible to understand you perfectly! What the other person does, in fact, is interpret what you say through his or her own perception; that is, the other person's ability and capacity to understand. That person does not see the exact picture as you may see it. That person isn't you! It also may be surprising to find out that a friend may understand your words or actions better than your spouse at times. Maybe that's because your friend has taken what you have said at face value, thinking that you mean exactly what you've said. Your spouse, on the other hand, may tend to read between the lines, interpreting your words partly based on past conversations or experiences.

I believe loving is the total leaving of yourself in order to completely understand another person. It is when we leave ourselves, our consciousness, and take that of Christ that we are in true harmony with Him. It is when we deny ourselves, when we lose our lives for Him, that we find our true lives. Each person should learn to read the other without "reading between the lines." Reading between the lines has a tendency to spoil things. Almost everyone is guilty of this. Human beings are *basically* self-inclined. We bring our personalities (the essence of ourselves) into everything—talks, feelings, situations, and circumstances. We have a greater desire to be understood than to understand. We only *half* listen to the other person while they talk.

But we can have the peace and harmony we seek in our relationships if we can learn to leave ourselves completely and take time to study and understand the other person. In serving one another and fulfilling each other's dreams and desires, we will actually ease the problems in our relationships and have our dreams coming true as well! It has got to be a mutual thing, though, not one-sided. Wouldn't it be wonderful if two parties could do this at the same time—together? Neglect and lack of communication, as we have said earlier, can undermine the quality of a relationship.

There is a need for assurance in a relationship. It should be felt *and* known. Always say what you feel no matter how often that is. If not, you may find the other party slowly drifting away. It happens, no matter how much you may *claim* to love and *know* each other. Oh, it may take years, but it will eventually happen because human beings are mortal and that's the way it goes. Anything can happen right under your nose in a week, in a month, or in a year. When separated by long distance, letters and phone calls are *necessary*. This is why married people can drift apart when travel is involved. Young married people full of love in their early years can sacrifice themselves to understand and keep in tune, but later on, they live out their lives ignorant of their partners. Their *own* personalities become exhibited more.

So in marriage or in friendship it should constantly be an *exchange* of selves and a respect for the other person's ideas and views. Constant communication is necessary. Don't assume! Be *freshly related* even if you have known your friend or spouse for years and you've gone through a lot together. These mistakes and misunderstandings can occur because the other person is actually reading you or the situation through their own personality or what they are feeling at that particular moment. You are bound to have these glitches at times without even being aware of it. You think the person is interpreting your messages all the time, *rightly* and *correctly*. Oh, how misleading this can be!

A word, letter, or call could come just in time to save you from a bad situation or difficult temptation! Everyone is prone to temptation, but "secured" in love, you would be better able to *resist* and not fall. Learn to loosen up and talk. Don't hide. Speak your mind, bare your heart, and don't be afraid, even at the risk of being trodden or taken for granted. It can save your relationship.

While the other person is being cautious, let down your pride. You can save the situation.

Engaged singles should keep reading to better understand how this works in platonic relationships. This is so important for the success of your courtship and relationship. You need to know one another—your faults and fears, your weaknesses, ambitions, and beliefs. This knowledge should not be clouded by emotion. It should be realistic enough to acknowledge who the other person is—faults and all.

To marry is a decision. *Emotions are not decisions.* Friendships that last involve a commitment. It takes a decision to make a great relationship work.

The Senses

The five sense organs can cause a crisis if allowed to be a distraction. They're broken down easily.

Sight

Girls love handsome and rich men, characteristics they can see *visibly*. If you are so inclined, set your *mind* and your eyes on quality. Character is the *evidence* of a handsome man, the most important evidence. Men who love looking a lot with their mouths agape and pounding hearts should try and restrain their eyes. Remember that quality is what really counts. Someone may look fine but have a nasty temper. Even if the person looks nice, ask yourself this question: "Would this person help me in my Christian growth, in things that have value and are constructive?" This should be your objective. Don't just settle for someone who soothes your loneliness and the pride of the *eye*.

You should also refuse to be of that type that flaunts a beautiful girlfriend or handsome boyfriend. Please be someone of value and intelligence. The things that matter in life are not always those things that glitter. If you want quality, I believe God *will* give it to you. Just be patient. Your dreams can come true.

Being in God's ministry and doing what God wants you to do does not mean you should not be ambitious. I believe you can make it, if you are willing to work hard to achieve your goals rather than ride on someone else's coat tails. And never become dependent on another person's money. Don't long for it. Instead, have the courage to make your own. God has called you *separately* and has made you an individual.

If, however, the things you see affect you a lot, *remove* your eyes. In other words, remove yourself from the presence of that person or thing. Don't stay there! Your body and mind will automatically digest what your eyes feed on. There may be people who aren't affected by the things they see, but don't say you want to toughen yourself up to belong to that group. Don't deceive yourself. What is sin is sin. What is lustful is lustful. Don't let provocative, tempting things linger and get imprinted in your mind. Withdraw yourself. If you watch too many romantic films, or worse yet provocative or pornographic films, your body will definitely react! Don't act tough. You are likely to dream in the night or have wet dreams!

You can cultivate the *habit* of feeding your eyes if you are not careful. You will become enslaved to the lust of the eye. The eye feeds the mind *faster* than most sense organs in the body.

Hearing

What you hear also stimulates your sensual desires. When you hear over and over how sweet you are, it makes you feel fine, doesn't it? When you associate yourself with friends who have no common goals with you but talk easy, be warned! What they say is bound to set you thinking and imagining. Their words sink subtly into your soul. Don't listen to things that are bound to make you go astray. Tell them to stop filling your head with rubbish, or better yet, stop seeing those people. Remove your-self. Don't be around them, just like Joseph ran from Potiphar's wife. (See Genesis 39:12.)

Don't waste your time with people whose speech is not uplift-ing. If they are prone to obscene language, engage in destructive gossip, and chase after vain dreams, you should not get involved with them! Be realistic. The things you hear should be constructive, beautiful, and worthy of your calling. Faith comes by *hearing*. Hear-ing is listening. Don't forget that. And hearing comes by the Word of God. So, love, lust, hate, and envy can come through hearing as well! Listening can be constructive or destructive. Make sure you are listening to the right things.

Touch

Touching is dangerous even for the *mature* single. This is one area girls love. They may not want the real thing—sex—but they want to be touched! They long to be cuddled, but unfortunately, men do not want to stop at holding hands. They usually want more. Touch-ing arouses them, while for girls it provides a feeling of security, love, warmth, and compassion.

Touching can make both boys and girls feel something they never have felt before or intended to feel. Touching is a commu-nication. It is reaching out to something or someone. Touching on its own is beautiful, unless it is extended to caressing. Some people need to touch you to know if they are communicating. It is like a gesture to them. As they talk, they gently touch you with their hands as they explain and exchange views with you.

However, one ought to know the difference between touching and caressing. Touching doesn't usually cause arousal, but a caress may. When someone exceeds the limits of touching and starts fondling, you should not assume your senses are stiff and dead. Your body's reactions should warn you of the danger ahead. So be careful about hugs and kisses if your body starts reacting violently.

Maintain clean relationships with a sound mind, and you will be all right. Think right. To the pure, all things are pure. Your limits should come from the Spirit, so be wise.

Taste and Smell

Are you having problems with eating? Do you feel you have slowly become a glutton? Your god has become your belly in a way. It started with your taste buds, then smell and appetite. You eat everything you see. Everything that smells nice, you feel like eating. If you cannot control your reaction to the smell of a good food in your nostrils, stop going to restaurants or shops. Take the other way. Stop tasting everything you see. You must learn self-control. Learn *discipline.* Self-control is one of the fruits of the Spirit that abides in you, so it is possible, quite possible, for you to control your eating habits. (See Galatians 5:22-25.) Self-control also means long-suffering so be *long-suffering* in your desire to discipline your consumption of food. Get back on your diet and don't give up.

Beauty

You and everyone on this earth have been wonderfully and beautifully made. (See Psalm 139:14.) I believe strongly that there are no ugly humans on the face of the earth. Everything has been exquisitely made with such diversity. There are different heights, shapes, and sizes—tall, stout, short, round, square, oblong bodies and faces. All Africans are beautiful, and so are the Indians, Americans, Eskimos, Chinese, Britons, and Australians. People of every race and nation are beautiful.

When you look at faces, see the detail. Some seem carved out with boldness, others, delicately done. Nothing created is ugly, but rather a great work of art. *A creative creation.* The short, stout person is beautiful. That person with the bald head is beautiful. There is no ugliness, just differences. It is a *form.*

I personally derive pleasure from watching human beings, their shapes and their sizes, how they move, act, and react. We are all truly beautiful—those with big round eyes and those with small engraved eyes half hidden in their sockets. It is as if they're keeping a secret! Thick lashes, thin brows, nothing is by chance. God has planned it all, no matter how incongruous it might seem. It makes each of us all the more rare and wonderful! Take a look at the mirror and discover all your unique and beautiful qualities.

The world has its typical ideas about what beauty is, but it can't see beauty like the Creator does. Take a look at the nose. Some are big and flare majestically. Others have narrow bridges and stand proud, while some are simply shorter. The big elephant ears and small trumpet ears are all truly beautiful and unique! There are big, full, sensuous mouths and small thin ones, delicately molded. Some people have short, muscled legs that look like yams that denote strength and power, even in women. All these things are beautiful because they are a unique creation, a fusion of different articles, different in shape, some contrasting, some complementary.

The problem comes when you decide to distort your body with anorexia, obesity, and implants of different sorts. It's your house. Keep it clean for your Master, Jesus. He won't mind you keeping house for Him.

I can go on and on and express beauty in all its ramifications. Beauty has many features—the face, the breasts, the hands, the bottom. It's the truth. Learn to love *yourself*. Love your features. We have been created by the Master Artist. The God who created the universe also created you. Would He say to you, "Son, daughter, you are awful. I must have made a mistake"? Of course not. God doesn't make mistakes. In fact, God looked over all He had created and declared that it was good. (See Genesis 1:25,27.)

Appreciate your beauty whether people think it is the *conventional* type of beauty or not. Trying to change things is risky. You will simply keep adjusting till there's no skin to stretch anymore. Age will creep up on you, no matter what. Death is a certainty. It's useless to try to retain your youth or look like someone else other than yourself. Instead, learn to appreciate your own special, peculiar features. Forget about yearning for somebody else's features! *Love your own.*

Learn to wear clothes that enhance your beauty. Learn the secrecy of your features. Don't criticize the way others look either. They are beautiful in their way as well. Thank God you feel you are beautiful! But know that no human face is ugly. Each has been touched by the Master Creator.

People often have a certain, subconscious perception of beauty that hinders them from seeing their own. Maybe they want to be six feet tall with broad shoulders or have long, straight legs and long, flowing hair. Don't worry about what you aren't. Appreciate what you are!

Listen, if no one praises you, praise yourself! Blow your own trumpet. Slowly but surely, someone will notice and appreciate what they see. That's how fashion evolves, you know! Someone starts wearing a certain style of clothing, and after awhile, others notice. Invent your own style! Be consistently yourself. I've even heard that when enough people praise it, even something once considered ugly can be transformed into something beautiful. So don't lose courage. Never do. You are beautiful. Everybody is.

I love it when I see someone's inner beauty and radiance shinning through, the result of being beautiful on the inside. It's impossible to be ugly on the outside. We can only be ugly on the inside! Can you see that? Jesus said some have eyes but cannot see. (See Matthew 13:15; Isaiah 6:9-10.) People are ugly because their inner nastiness shows through. Make your character beautiful, and you will have the most beautiful covering of all. (That's how to beat the world's idea of conventional beauty.) A jewel is appreciated by real people. Anyone who does not appreciate your inner beauty isn't worth a second thought!

Having considered the above, it should also be said that the entirety of beauty is not complete until we look to Jesus and His type. We are God's type of beauty, remember? His type of beauty is contagious and eternal. His type of beauty does not fade. Have you ever wondered if Jesus was handsome? This is what we read concerning Him in Isaiah 53:2-3, "He had no form or majesty that we should look at Him, nothing in His appearance that we should desire Him. He was despised and rejected by others; a man of suffering and acquainted with infirmity; and as one from whom others hide their faces, He was despised, and we held Him of no account" (NRSV).

Has anyone ever said that there is nothing in your appearance to be desired? Those who say so are blind. The same was said of Jesus. How untrue. Have you ever been despised and rejected because of your appearance? What a mistake! Jesus is a true gem, and He is not despised by those who know value when they see it. Have you suffered and are you acquainted with infirmity so that others hide their faces from you? How inadequate our sensibility, how numb? The Bible says Jesus was acquainted with infirmity and they ignorantly hid their faces from Him and held Him of no account!

Isaiah 52:14 tells us, "So marred was His appearance, beyond human semblance, and His form beyond that of mortals" (NRSV). Yet, Jesus is the most desired, most handsome, most sought after, and most loved by all who call upon the name of the Lord.

Psalm 45:2-4 says:

> *You are the most handsome of all. Gracious words stream from your lips. God Himself has blessed you forever. Put on your sword, O mighty warrior! You are so glorious, so majestic! In your majesty, ride out to victory, defending truth, humility, and justice. Go forth to perform awe-inspiring deeds!* (NLT)

Jesus is, indeed, most handsome as He rides out to victory, defending truth, humility, and justice and performing awe-inspiring deeds. Do you go out and perform such deeds? Do gracious words stream from your lips? You are beautiful then. Extremely so. Glorious and majestic in appearance. Now, can you fit all these descriptions together? Can the world? God can, and so can we. That's beauty. Know beauty as it ought to be. Jesus has set the standard we walk by.

8
Sex

What is sex for you? Is it proof that you are human and normal? Do you think of it as a right you have over another? Maybe you see it as a way to prove a point to everyone that no one can beat you, you are the best. You could see it as a tool to be used to show off your masculinity and stroke your ego. Do you see it as a way for a woman to have power over a man? Could you imagine it as something to exchange for services or money? Maybe sex to you is a way to escape reality or an outlet for all your pent-up thoughts and fantasies. You might even think of sex as an evil that must be endured or feared. Maybe you see it as a negative necessity.

What is sex to you? Any of the above?

For most people, sex is a pleasure. But it's important to have a clear view of what it is all about, its place in our lives. We need to better understand its nature and its use in order to adequately enjoy and understand it. We are talking about sex here because some singles do have sexual problems as we have previously discussed. As well, some single Christians may have vowed to remain single due to the misconceived idea of sex as sin—apart from the negative assumptions and fear of sex.

Sex is a *divine gift* given to man for expression, not as a means to an end! When we express ourselves, we communicate our thoughts and feelings to someone else. It is a gift because it *gives* pleasure, has *potential,* and *satisfies.* It is a gift because of its many nice abilities! Gifts are given to those who can take care of them. This gift will hold you accountable, so don't be too hasty to accept it!

Sex is not wholly for procreation. Couples should feel free to indulge in it after their children have been born. Sex is about intimacy because it involves being vulnerable to another person and sharing desires. It's about trusting that other person. Why is it not just for procreation? You must note that when a person is in love, he or she yearns to move closer to that loved one—to touch and hold and cuddle that other person. The thing being expressed here is not necessarily the desire to have a child. Most of the time, that doesn't even come to mind. Rather, it is an expression of a desire to share and merge with that loved one. (See Genesis 2:23–25.) How this is to be done should be left to instinct. Loving one another boils down to sex. Touching and cuddling heads toward it. In marriage there are no holds barred! They ought to merge. Adam said so! (See Genesis 2:23.)

The Gift of Sex

The gift of sex, therefore, should be treated with care and not misused. This gift is from the One who created you and your sexual organs and desires. Now our Creator says, "Marriage is honorable among all, and the bed undefiled" (Hebrews 13:4 NKJV). There are no hard and fast rules concerning this. The misuse of sex has resulted in syphilis, gonorrhea, VD, herpes, and AIDS. It's no use side-stepping the issue. The abuse of sex has also resulted in emotional damage. Self-esteem has been distorted, mental wounds inflicted apart from physical wounds. Sex, when given its proper place, can be enjoyed. Through sex, you can actually express feelings of tenderness, gentleness, assertiveness, compassion, and many others. This should be reserved for the one you feel such intense emotions for. Not just anyone, not every Tom, Dick, and Harry! That is promiscuity.

Love, Sex, and Discipline

To love is a decision of the head and heart. It is not just an emotion. Sex is meant to communicate at a deeper physical and emotional level exactly what you are feeling. Sex, like love, requires discipline. For love, you discipline your heart, wisely building your relationship, forgiving one another even when you don't feel like it, making time for each other, accommodating each other on issues that are suitable for Christians. But sex requires discipline, as well. We have said that the body reacts to stimuli. It can react to someone you don't love! Sex between novices can be improved as talking and sharing increase. As you learn to open up to each other and not be so inhibited, you will find more and more joy together. Sex requires patience as well. (Please read *Love and Life* by Leonie McSweeney.)

Why is sex called lovemaking? The overriding ingredient in married sex is love, not lust. It is not self-making or bodymaking, but lovemaking. It is called lovemaking because it is a *shared knowledge* of love. However, it takes *trust* to be able to express your sexual desires. If you don't trust one another, you could be hindered. Trust your spouse and express your sexual desires. In this way, you will have less temptation to stray outside your marriage or live your lifetime *wondering* how it would have felt had you been able to let go and express yourself. Please, single adults, don't experiment—this gift was meant for married life! If you are already involved in an affair, recognize your mistake and *get out*.

Lovemaking should not be used to prove a point. It belittles sex as a love communication and expression. Nor should you use it to hold your mate! One day it will wear off. Someone out there can do it just like you, if not better. Don't kid yourself. Your hold is only temporary. Even so, you are using it as a tool. Let your character, your personality be the real asset the other person sees. Show that person your valuable habits and abilities. Prove your love in the right ways. Sex comes later.

However, let us not play down the role of sex in a person's life. It is necessary for the human soul. We have physical bodies and these bodies should be nurtured! Its needs are basic. They stem from emotions we feel that come from the heart. Sex strengthens already *healthy* relationships. If the relationship is not healthy, sex will eventually destroy it.

In a healthy marriage, it is acceptable for husbands and wives to express their desires and fantasies to each other. These fantasies should not come from pornographic books or films and should always show respect for the other partner. Let your wife or husband have enough trust in you to be able to express his or her desires to you without shame. You are simply hindering your spouse if you care only about your own desires.

You would-be wives should know that husbands need sex. It strengthens them and enhances their sense of *togetherness*! Love-making ought not to decline after the first few years. Sex should be enjoyed throughout life. Women, don't cast it aside once your children have been born. (See Matthew 19:5-6.) This is a mistake many have made. Try it after a quarrel when you have both made up. Don't go to bed as platonic lovers! Sex brings in a new freshness, mystery, and eroticism your marriage needs. Husbands may get tired of pressuring you. Sometimes they press subtly. Most times you might not even be aware of what they want! Also, don't turn a deaf ear or pretend! Stop grumbling. Remember, the word is *love*—before the making!

Men ought not to demand sex without "preparing the ground." Women are moved by sentiments, words, and touch. They love gifts (it's just their nature!). After marriage, men often stop doing these little things women love and think their wives will gladly welcome them anyway. Women need to be stimulated first through their emotions. When they are softened up, they will melt like butter. That is the key to good sex!

Christians, we ought to be the best of married couples when we get married. We have enough resources, material, and knowledge to be so. I wish all single adults that wish to get married the best—as much as I wish those who want to remain unattached the best. Keep yourself under control, don't burn with lust. Meanwhile, remember your duty lies in First Corinthians 7:20, which says, "Let each one remain in the same calling in which he was called" (NKJV).

Lovemaking Allowed?

How many single Christians can honestly abstain from lovemaking? All single adults should at least try! Most simply *just haven't tried*. They have taken it as a natural function. What a shame! What will they have left to share when it is time to wed their spouse? Some single adults need contact, a touch, physical reassurance. Those who are engaged or in a close relationship feel it is all right to indulge in kissing and petting. They build a small fire. But not many have the strength of character to quench the fire before it turns into a "burning bush." Look, it is better to be *dead* peacefully than alive in flames! Of course, "dead" here means not knowing, being ignorant about these feelings, and "alive in flames" means the calories you would have lost and the tortures of the sexual experience.

Sex is the highest level of expression, a total giving of yourself to your partner. Sex should involve not only your body but also your mind and soul. A very close relationship with anyone can prompt the desire in some to share and bare themselves to their partner.

Understand that sex is a divine gift given to man from God for expression. Understand, too, that sharing should only be for one other soul. This was God's ultimate plan when He made one Eve for one Adam. He did not introduce two Eves to Adam. He knew one would satisfy him and be sufficient for him physically, mentally, and emotionally. She was his sole companion and partner. (See Genesis 2:22.) Your wife will be that kind of helpmate to you also if you are faithful to her. (See Genesis 2:18, Psalm 5:15-20.)

It should equally be noted that God did not make another man to keep Adam company and to mate with him. God didn't make Steve to mate with Steve—instead, God made a mirror of a *different* type. He gave Adam an Eve, a woman. Homosexuals and lesbians have missed it.

Now let's review!

Kissing can be looked at as an expression solely from the heart. Some single Christians who are in love find it hard to abstain from it. We know that most of the time, women need a lot of touching, not necessarily sex! It comforts and reassures them that they are loved. Unfortunately, some men misunderstand this need in women and demand more. Lovemaking as an expression can be in the words you use when you speak to one another—words that smile—or in holding hands. We should be clean from the heart and have clean intentions for our spouse or loved one. Men should be protective of women. They should not want to ravage them. They are not the wolves outside. If an *unbeliever* ravages them and you do, too, what hope is there? When you love someone, bear in mind that the person will be yours *forever* because you are going to marry the person! So be faithful.

Men, don't kiss women randomly. Kissing, my friend, is an exchange, a promise! What's the matter with you? Why kiss them and promise them nothing? Kissing can be a habit, easy to pick up but difficult to drop. It becomes your level of communication. Don't string women along by simply satisfying your passions. This shows you have no character and discipline. You are a cheat.

And women, if you are on such intimate terms with a man and he has not mentioned anything honorable or formally asked for your hand in marriage, you are a fool to continue that relationship. Don't hold on. You can drag a horse to water, but you can't make him drink. Your relationship should be specific and defined. At least there must be some solid direction. Don't live on hopes and dreams. Don't float; say things and mean them. Oh, ye children of God!

True Intimacy

Our bodies are the temples where God abides. Let us treat them with awe, honor, and respect. Know that the woman in your life is God's own and of great value. She deserves your respect. The same goes for women. Know that the man in your life is of great value. He deserves your respect. Don't keep him on the hook. Don't tease him, either for material or emotional gain. Be straight in your dealings.

One sure way is to be intimate platonic friends with the person you love. This should be first and foremost. Sex can be platonic, remember? You can express yourselves fully in these ways. "Make love" that way! Search the other person's mind. Look at his or her character. Truly get to know that person as a friend. Find out what makes your special person tick. Learn to communicate even in silence. Let your expression not rest solely on the lovemaking that should be reserved for marriage. Learn to be fulfilled with the sharing of minds. Be close enough to know when the other person is flagging spiritually. Get in the habit of praying for each other. Do your part to avoid pressure and temptation. Sometimes abstaining from physical expression can help.

Remember, there is no hurry if he or she is going to one day be yours. Don't deceive yourselves, but keep yourselves pure. Don't lust. The key to your behavior is to *remember* that you are God's own children.

9
FEARS HARBORED—VIRGIN OR NOT

Who is a virgin in the eyes of God? The answer, dear one, is a person who is pure in heart and body. Whether you are technically a virgin or not, once you are pure in heart and determined to keep your body pure *from that time on*, you are a *reasonable* sacrifice to the Lord. (See Romans 12:1-2.) And for this, you *are* a virgin—to God. The past has been wiped away, forgiven and forgotten. You have a *new* record. Your thoughts and life have been transformed. You transform it by the renewing of your mind with His Word. You are a new, sinless creature. Whether you were a whore, had abortions, even if you did these things once, twice, ten times, you became a virgin from the day you gave up your life of corruption and immorality—to God. You are now clean. Correct your thinking. In God's eyes, He sees you this way, whether you are a man or a woman.

Some people can be technically virgins but be unclean inside. Some perform unclean sexual acts and yet pride themselves that they are virgins. Some do so without a qualm of guilt. They are no better. God is interested in *purity* of heart and your *sensitivity* to Him. Who do you spend time with? Bad company *can* influence and corrupt you. Slowly you would wither away without realizing it. Stay pure and be assured in your heart. You are God's own. (See Psalm 82:5-6; Second Corinthians 5:17.)

Some Few...

Some know God loves and wants them to remain unattached for *now*. Some even know God would want them to be single for some time *to come*, but they fear the cost. The price they must pay seems impossible. It looms larger than life before their eyes. These things are not spoken, only thought of and dreaded. They are *hidden* in some men and women. But I believe in these end times, *all* gifts from God should be exhibited. God is coming to rapture a glorious and mature Church. I understand the fear or the price you think you cannot pay. You see God moving you in such a direction, and you wonder why? You don't want to carry that great responsibility. However, the gift of being single has its own compensations.

Consider this. Virtue would literally flow out of you. Your body, your being will *ooze out* power and radiance. Your *children* will be more than the *sands* of the sea. Nothing you say *"can fall down to the ground."* (See First Samuel 3:19.) Indeed it shall not, it cannot fall. I know the fear of this responsibility, which many shy away from or turn a blind eye to. Well, you will be able to pay such a price if it's for you. God will make it possible for you to *withstand the loneliness for companionship and its temptations.* You won't even have to struggle! You would rather find yourself struggling to have or keep a relationship. Even the thought of an *erotic, intimate relationship will repulse you.*

You will find out you cannot stay in a confined relationship. You will *not find rest* in one. Instead of welcoming it, your heart will reject it. You will feel so *caged* in, with a constant *burning* desire *to be free.* To be free would seem to be "whole" to you. You would desire to be free with ease, *without regrets.* It's not that you don't love relationships. No! You treasure them, but you've become a *relationship within* yourself that exceeds the *confinements* of the marriage type. Only a few will fully understand this. It would take *only* you to fully *understand* and *know* that you are to be a eunuch or to be single and unattached. You understand love and not the *absence* of it. You are not afraid of *loving* either. Most times, however, note that this period of being a eunuch is for a period of time set out by God. Some are for a short period, some longer, and a few are for life. You will know which is yours.

Have no fear. As long as this continues, flow in its power, ability, and knowledge. *Relax*. In time you may be allowed by the Holy Spirit and be fully free *within* your spirit to love someone in the *eros* way (physical intimacy). Don't force it. Don't destroy its uniqueness. It may be strange to many, but so *secure* and *real* to you. So please don't worry. Remember your ability does not mean a *disability*. You love others very deeply. There is no problem with your heart!

Everything has a price, my dear, whether you are single or married. If you cannot pay the price of being unattached for a long time or for a lifetime, rest assured that God will not ask that of you. He will not ask you to do something that is too much for you to bear. "No testing has overtaken you that is not common to everyone. God is faithful, and He will not let you be tested beyond your strength, but with the testing He will also provide the way out so that you may be able to endure it" (1 Cor. 10:13 NRSV).

Reasons Some Choose to Remain Single

The choice to remain single often comes after a long period of spinsterhood or bachelorhood, separation, or widowhood. You can no longer tolerate or adapt to another person, no matter how much you might *long* to marry. You are used to depending on yourself, making your own decisions. Your desires and wants have always been under your control. You may feel it is impossible to enter wholeheartedly into any relationship. To put it another way, "your eyes are now wide open." It is good to have open eyes and an open heart, but it is equally good to be quick to forgive and able to tolerate others. In this condition, you may not make a good wife or husband, because marriage is all about tolerating and sharing. You are not used to sharing your emotions, your thoughts, or yourself. Some people can make good friends, good girlfriends or boyfriends, but not good husbands or wives, unless they readjust their attitudes and values. Some of you have, however, transferred or channeled all your emotions to the Lord and the things of God. If so, your single life can be very beautiful. If you have not broken your bond with God, you can go a long way.

But if you have been *crippled* before, that is, fallen in love with someone, it would be a difficult road to continue as uncommitted and single for life. This is *because* such desires and knowledge are bound to arise again and again. Each time, you will be weakened. A piece of yourself will be given away. Your desire to remain unattached may wane and become worse if you eventually give in to *erotic* relationships, only to come out again and again. You would eventually reach a state of confusion, not knowing what you want anymore. As such, it is better to take a step back, evaluate your desires, and position yourself critically before making up your mind. Tell God what you *really* want, not what you desire or *dream* of being. It may be time. Only then can you continue properly with your life.

Your reason for wanting to live the single life might be because you want to prove something to God out of a sense of love and devotion. This is all right in itself, but my advice is this: Continue in your marital status as long as *this* singular resolve to belong wholly to God and work for His kingdom *lasts*. Listening to other people concerning this will only *complicate* the issue and could cause you to fall into snares of sin largely due to a confused mind. You may want to *try out* things you have had no desire for in the past. Continue on your pathway until you're no longer truly desirous to remain unattached and your resolve is waning. By this time, you would have *blazed* a trail, an achievement few can match in a lifetime with such purity, devotion, and love for the Lord. The Lord your God will surely commend you. He is the one who gives you the strength and grace to stick to your guns.

However, remember that if and when the time of waning comes, cry out and say, "God, I am weary. Search me and see, hear my heart's cry!" He *will* listen. You have not disappointed Him. You are telling Him *how* you feel. And if and when the time comes for a partner, *don't struggle* for so long! It is beautiful to marry; both are *gifts* from God, given by God. In both, you can ultimately serve God. You only have to marry someone with your zeal, beliefs, dreams, and love for the Lord. Don't settle for less. God would love to have two peas in a pod. Be of good cheer. Your desire for singleness is not *weird*. If only you knew how much God desires one of such strength and purpose. God is looking for men and women who *without* fear can *step* out, all-conquering, into His vision for them. He looks for men and women who would *dare* step forward with their hearts on their sleeves for Him, comfortable with whatever is to come!

Some Christian singles may desire to remain single because of some mistake or sin they committed in the past. This is probably a nagging, besetting sin that has clung to them for a long time. Oh, dear one, God sees your heart and your love. Don't worry. Just love Him and do all He asks of you. That is all *He asks* of you, *not* all *you ask* of Him. You don't have to prove anything to Him except to obey Him and *stop* sinning. To stop sinning, you must depend on His grace. He says His grace is sufficient for you and if He says so, it is true. You can and you do have the ability. If not, He would not have said so or asked it of you. He knows you can do without this besetting sin. It may take a while, but you can do it! Keep your heart and mind on Him. Let Him guard your heart. He believes in your ability to get through this.

If it is a past sin, *let it go*! The kind of sin that gets this type of vow of *"abstinence"* is the sex sin, homosexuality and fornication. (See First Corinthians 6:13-20.) It is typically a sin that is within the body, the temple of God. This is why most Christian singles decide to serve God with their bodies without marrying. They feel guilt that they did not continue to be a virgin before marriage and now wish to be a virgin for God by not marrying. Many singles feel this way after becoming born again.

Don't think this way. Understand that before God you are a virgin because you are a born-again Christian. That is what matters. You became a sweet aroma when you surrendered your life totally to Him. When you gave up immorality and repented, He washed you clean with His blood. You don't *have* to prove it to Him by being forever celibate. You are sweet to Him, and He sees your love. However, you may continue if you have made this vow to God, because I know it is difficult to let go of a vow especially when made with devotion, sincerity, and purity of heart. If you feel it is right, go ahead. God will teach you so many things. But if ever the time comes, and you find yourself falling off your decision again and again and your desire dims, tell God all about it so that He can direct you. Afterward, whatever it is, listen to your heart.

So let God be your guide, *not* man, sin, or circumstance. Some Christians wish to remain single because they have been influenced by books they have read, a film they've watched, or testimonies they've heard favoring singleness. Now, I don't mind the positive effect of a God-inspired book that gives an individual the push to ultimately use and get the best of his or her singlehood. Such influence should rightly challenge us to make the best of being unattached or single. As far as this motivation drives you, make the best of it. Don't cast it aside *without* doing your best by it. Blaze your trail so that all men may see the glory of God. When you look back in later years, you will have no regrets. You won't feel you have left anything undone that you should have done.

Thank you for using this beautiful gift of being single and unattached and blazing forward to see God's righteousness and the coming of His Kingdom. There is nothing done in vain for Him when it comes from the purity of your heart.

The Future

Some unattached Christian individuals are afraid of the future. They worry that if they don't marry now, they are going to lose out for good. They get the notion that they are incomplete unless married or at least engaged! This philosophy is completely wrong. No where in the Scriptures does it say you are incomplete unless married or engaged. In fact, Colossians 2:10 says, "Ye are complete in Him [Christ]." Removing a rib from Adam did not mean he was *no longer* complete. God created *perfect* beings, not half or incomplete ones. Adam was a complete human when God created him. God recognized that he had a need and filled that need with Eve. Even in reshaping your character, God does not leave you incomplete. No! Everything He does is done in perfection and completeness. Completeness comes with the Spirit! We are *one spirit* with God. *One* signifies wholeness; it is a *whole* figure. We are complete in Him.

Ask yourself what God wants from you and how you can work *ultimately* for Him. That's what you're supposed to be doing. God then requires you to listen absolutely to Him and work ultimately at your best. Adam *chose* to listen to the voice of his wife *rather* than God. "Then to Adam He said, 'Because you have heeded the voice of your wife'" (Gen. 3:17 NKJV). God informed Adam that his disobedience had brought a curse on the earth and things would be much more difficult for everyone because of it.

Eve chose to listen to the voice of satan. It is important that in things concerning God, husbands should listen to God, especially if their wives are telling them something different. No man should allow emotion to cloud his decisions concerning God's rules. I believe God has given both genders the responsibility of *discerning* His voice and obeying it. Life would be easier and much more beautiful if each listened to God first before each other or anyone else for that matter. Obeying Him actually promotes love, honesty, and safety. Obedience here is better than sacrifice. (See First Samuel 15:22.)

A single or unattached individual should show forth the dignity of God. (See First Timothy 4:12.) People should respect the phrase "I'm a born-again Christian" rather than "I am married." They should not ask your married status to *gauge* your character or sense of responsibility. Marriage should not be the yardstick to determine how you would react to situations and circumstances.

Unattached Christians should not want to be married because they think it would be *lovely* to sleep with someone all the time or live with a companion. There is more to mating and marriage than meets the eye. You are marrying another person, a different personality with a ministry uniquely created by God. Besides, you are not just marrying to keep yourself safe so that you will not commit fornication. Without self-control, you will commit adultery when married! Practice self-control now. It is one of the fruits of the Spirit. (See Galatians 5:22.) You will still need it when and if you marry. Marriage is a *different* institution from the one you are in now if single, so begin to enjoy your status. God said, "Seek ye first the kingdom of God, and His righteousness; and all these things shall be added unto you" (Matt. 6:33). The Revised Standard Version says those things "shall be yours as well"! As you are involved in the Master's business, He will care for you. Remember, His concern is for you.

Let no one despise your youth or resolve if you're unattached. Be an example. Be joyful that you are operating within your gift and anointing no matter how short or long it may be. God will take care of you. Spend your time *learning* and *understanding* your gift, dreaming and conquering for the Lord as you remain unattached. It would be unthinkable for those of you who have waited *so long* to get your heart's desire in a partner, to blow it and settle for a less deserving person (someone below your standards). I am not saying you shouldn't be realistic, but keep this quote about Esther in mind. She said, "If I perish, I perish" (Esther 4:16). Be like Shadrach, Meshach, and Abednego, who would not bow to or serve other gods. (See Daniel 3:16-18.)

Whether you are rescued or not, continue on the pathway the Lord has set for you. You and the Lord make an unbeatable team! Be strong.

The Fear of Normalcy

There is nothing as deadly for a Christian as the effects of *normalcy* in his or her life. What the world considers "normal" slowly *waters* everything down. You could slowly become a bulldog without teeth, full of knowledge *yet* powerless. As you involve yourself with the affairs of this world, the normal and natural things, you no longer feel like meeting with the brethren! Then a *dryness* seeps in. It's a subtle process. It seeps in, here and there, and begins to take root. Soon, you begin to feel like *fellowshiping* just with *yourself*. After all, God is with you! You have put in many years in the Lord, and you know so much already. Now you want a change, maybe a wild party! You'd settle for just about anything *normal* that will take your mind off spending time talking or fellowshiping with the Lord.

Your music collection increasingly comes from the *secular* section. You feel you've been concerned about the *supernatural* for too long. The books you read are no longer the edifying kind. Not only are they secular novels but extremely provocative as well, literature igniting lasciviousness. Some downright pornography. In fact, you're through with Christian books. You find them boring! Your attendance at midweek fellowship wanes, and Sunday services become an effort. You are hardly involved in church activities at all anymore. You've let all your church responsibilities go. The company you keep tends to be worldly. You're tired of being a superhero. You just want to be normal. After all, shouldn't you relax and enjoy life like everyone else?

All these are symptoms of self and flesh that have pulled down many Christians. Our streets are full of *former* giants. They are where satan wants them now. He thinks, "If I can't kill them, I'll cripple them and get them off course." Listen, you can be *supernaturally—natural!* To be a Christian, living the life Christ wants you to live, can be as *normal* as breathing.

Talk to God as naturally as you would the *next* person. It isn't necessary to kneel. As you go about your life, talk about Him, just as you would talk about cars, places, people, girls, or any other everyday thing. It is *not* a duty. That may be why you waned! You looked upon it as a compulsory duty rather than what it is—a natural thing that comes from your innate ability. Ask yourself if your faith and your life are a duty. Let them come naturally from you. If you neglect the things of God, you will dampen your power and ability. Let it be natural for you to talk and fellowship with God. Let it become normal for you! It's natural because your nature comes from God. You're one with Him. This *natural* state then becomes *normal* for you.

If there is a gap in your communication with God, get up and step up. It is normal in the sequence of relationships for gaps to occur due to infiltrations. This should not alarm you. It happens in every relationship, with friends, parents, and spouses. But because the nature of God is natural in you, you will get back your fellowship with Him, so don't panic. So long as you make "your natural abilities" work as normal for you, there will be no problem. You will then be able to escape the normal things of this world that work against the nature of God. Your natural is based on your nature as a Christian. Normal comes from what you accept as an everyday occurrence and routine. The natural from this world comes from the nature and the normalcy of daily accepted routines.

Now "the flesh" walks in the normalcy of this world; that's the snag. If you give in to too much self or the flesh and its instincts, it will dominate and pull you under! Flesh walks with self. Jesus said that while the flesh is weak, the spirit is willing! (See Mark 14:38.) Jesus also wanted the cup of suffering to pass Him by at the Garden of Gethsemane. (See Mark 14:36.) He was fighting against His flesh and self with its propensity for the world. Let's always renew our minds with the Word of God. However, we are more than conquerors because we are in actuality spirits and the Spirit of God dwells in us. It is the Spirit who quickens. Hallelujah! (See Romans 8:11.)

You are a spirit being. Therefore, be conscious of your spirit self at all times. You will have times of refreshment, just as there will come times of dryness. These refreshments will come when the Lord prompts you to get up early in the morning without a struggle or effort and with a song in your heart. Obey these instincts; don't ignore them. That's the refreshing!

Refreshing may come from a Christian tract you've picked up and read or a moving sermon you've recently heard. Remember, in a day, there are mornings, afternoons, and nights. Mornings declare a new day breaking; afternoons are filled with work, and nights are designed to soothe our dry and weary bodies and minds with much-needed rest. These differences through the day depict the variations you see in your Christian walk and in your relationships. Thank God that we can always rest in Him. He is our Rest. Anytime you need it, turn to Him. Don't run away from Him and enter into other rests. They are false. It is His mercy, and His alone, that is new every morning.

During Noah's generation, it was the normalcy of that life that ensnared most of the people. I am sure they had time for refreshment, reflection, and a chance to change their minds. As morning broke each day, they had an opportunity to ponder Noah's words. But they didn't. God's Spirit of *mercy* was available and moving upon the earth before Noah finished the ark and closed the doors. But they decided to stay in the realm of normalcy around them.

Don't choose to stay neutral, untouched, and unmoved by God. There is no lasting joy in the thrilling things *of the world*, especially if you have tasted the goodness of the Lord. These happenings are fleeting and can never be compared to the joy of God's presence. You will only be half existing and in limbo. I believe when you surrender your consciousness to the reality of the presence of Jesus in your life, you can walk with Him as a way of life. It is possible to live naturally and normally in His presence.

Enoch walked with God and did not see death. (See Genesis 5:24.) He was taken up *bodily* to heaven because he walked *right* with God as a *natural,* normal thing to do. And he did so for 365 years! Elijah was also taken to heaven. He was a frail man and had many human weaknesses. He was *afraid* of Jezebel even after his conquest over Baal's 450 prophets. He was so afraid, in fact, that He ran away! (See First Kings 19:3-4.)

These men of God lived among people even before the Holy Spirit came to reside in the hearts of men, *empowering* them with the evidence of speaking in tongues, before the day of Pentecost. Be encouraged! If these men could live with God without falling along the wayside, you can survive and stay true to God. He who started a good thing in you will perform it and complete it—even until His coming. (See Philippians 1:6.) He is the one who "…worketh in you both to will and to do of His good pleasure" (Phil. 2:13).

Some Special Cases

There are those whose response to loving is *numbness*. They feel there is really no need to fall in love. It all feels to them like chasing the wind, and it takes so much energy and stamina. They feel it isn't worth it. If you are one of these people, you are not alone in your estimation. Millions of people out there feel the same way. Don't feel pressure to find someone to fall in love with you. Any relationship that feels like a burden should not be encouraged.

This emotional numbness may get worse as you get older. You lack energy to put into relationships as you age. Go for easy friendships. You have to be a friend before you can become engaged. Be yourself, be natural, and things will turn out fine. If you have someone you feel at ease with, someone who does not cause you stress, that proves there is nothing terribly wrong with you! Such easy relationships are actually what you need to loosen up and stop your fear. The love of God that floods your heart is easy to shoulder, isn't it? The love He wants you to share and radiate is not an effort for you either, is it? Look upon relationships *in this light*! Make friends you can relax with, laugh with, and be at ease with. Being with people you like doesn't require a lot of effort. Such people are easy to love.

Loving is not hard. Sometimes it's just the approach that causes friction. People with this type of numbness have most likely gone through some rough experience. This can be shattering and heartrending. Remember that God heals. Take easy steps and acknowledge them.

Continue loving Him and putting your conflicts, troubles, and grievances in His care. He will take care of you and make things come through for you. Paul the apostle, a man with an extraordinary mission, was mortal with mortal needs, afflictions, and disappointments. And yet he was capable of loving others greatly. He wrote most of the terms of love. (See First Corinthians 13.) He understood love in all its components; he even knew how it can be part of the single life! If you fall into this category and understand, love like this; don't be colored by *strife, stress, and misconceptions*. You can then zealously continue in your single status, while leaving open the door to marrying again.

Christians who have stood for a long time in the *intimacy* of the Lord can largely *withstand* the emotion of love called *eros*. Probably this is the reason they are so strong-minded in any resolve they have. They fear to trespass to a different pasture. Different pasture here may refer to a different marital status, position, or resolve. It all looks strange to them. Some feel that this could separate them from God's Kingdom and dampen the love for God in their hearts. Whenever there is a longing for a soulmate, a different position or marital status, or a change in environment, they feel *guilty and uneasy*!

If this is how you feel, God understands your conflict. You've come a long way with Him. If this condition becomes a *burden* to you, He does not want it so. He *understands* your love and thirst for Him. It should not cause a *war* in your heart, for there is *nothing* in the whole of creation that can *separate* you from the love of God. No depth, no height, things that are or things to come. (See Romans 8:31.)

The best thing to do is to talk to Him all the time as *each* conflict comes along. Let things take root before you eventually step out in whichever direction you want. Remember there is nothing He cannot do for you. If you choose to change your marital status or your position, don't be afraid or feel guilty about telling Him. He knows you will always choose to listen to His voice. God comes first! He's what matters. I believe it is good for every unattached Christian to have a healthy outlook on being single or married. Take your calling to a higher level. Dare to step out.

10
THE GIFT OF BEING SINGLE

Paul said in First Corinthians 7:7 that both being married and being single are *gifts*. These are gifts given to individuals and, therefore, should not be abused or misused or trod upon. We will be talking about the gift of being single here. If you are unmarried, single, separated, or widowed, you are *operating* within that gift. This is something you should be proud of.

We all know that Paul advised bishops and deacons to be husbands of one wife. This same Paul said for the sake of convenience that, "I wish that all men were even as I myself" (1 Cor. 7:7 NKJV). Paul wasn't married. And in verse 38 he says, "He who refrains from marriage will do better" (1 Cor. 7:38 NRSV). The summary for both married and unmarried can be found in First Corinthians 7:32-39, which says, "I want you to do whatever will help you serve the Lord best" (NLT).

In First Corinthians 7:6, Paul says, "I say this as a concession, not as a command" (NLT). Paul has the Spirit of God. He is not discrediting the married or the unmarried. He has a balanced view.

In First Corinthians 7:7, Paul says, "I wish everyone were single, just as I am. But God gives to some the gift of marriage, and to others the gift of singleness" (NLT). Gifts from God are bestowed to men from His very heart. Gifts are blessings. Eve was a blessing to Adam. The woman was God's gift to man. Women ought to be gifts to men, someone to bless them. Children are gifts to married couples, a blessing to their marriage. Talents are regarded as gifts as well. Presents are gifts. A gift gives its owner "contentment and joy" as well as the ability to accomplish great things.

God gives gifts, but I like the Good News Bible rendering of First Corinthians 7:7. It refers to this not just as a gift but as a "special gift." God says it is special to remain single or to be married! God gave us these special gifts because He believes that we can take care of them. Note: We walk in the *capacity* of *both* as *gifts* by His *grace*—the gift of marriage and the gift of being single.

Gifts from God *contain* grace. Grace *brings* ability, mercy, and forgiveness to continue and make things work. It's wonderful when we treasure a gift, preserve it, and take good care of it. When we regard something as a treasure, we are more inclined to look after it. Don't let your treasure lie there unused, and don't misuse it. Gifts in the natural realm are not given to those who don't appreciate them! God gives gifts because He trusts that you will not trample them under your feet. We are God's covenant children. Gifts are given to those He loves.

As gifts are intended to bring joy into your life, singleness (because it is a gift) should bring joy as well. Remember that good, careful, and disciplined people take care of their gifts. Those who misuse their gifts displease the giver. In those cases, the gifts aren't taken away, but those who receive the gifts exchange their joy for discontentment, dissatisfaction, and unhappiness. The gift's potential for good is lost.

Sometimes people bestow gifts on others, but they do it grudgingly. That is not our God. He freely and abundantly gives us His very best.

When you consider the gift of singleness, remember that it is something we all pass through in our lives. After all, none of us were born married. We all get a foretaste of what this gift is like.

Singleness is an eye-opener. It can help you learn and mature. In fact, it can be called the gift of self-discovery, a special time to learn about yourself, your personality. Everyone should experience this because it is an effective way to improve your *personal uniqueness* (those special qualities that make you who you are). The single status is enriching.

To be gifted, to a certain degree, means a person has a special ability. Those who are gifted need to prove their talent, demonstrating their skill in the gift that has been bestowed upon them. These people *go all the way* because of their gifts. They have the *ability* to do so. They have considerable *proficiency* and *competence* to achieve all that they desire using *whatever is* at their disposal. Circumstance, situations, people, and events are bent to suit *and* not hinder them.

If gifted, you have the aptitude to use your gift. It is *inherent* in you. Regarding the gift of being single, this means a person has also been given the disposition and an ease to learn and understand the life they've chosen. It is not a burden, though some on the outside looking in might think so.

Before marriage, most people enjoy a sense of freedom. Their achievements are real and theirs alone. This is such an important aspect of life that everyone is better off to have experienced a time of singleness before marriage. If we misuse or fail to appreciate the gift of singleness, we will not make the most of the gift of marriage. We all need a chance to discover who we are. In that regard, singleness is a guiding light, an important tool in our development. How disappointing it is that this gift is so often misunderstood and unappreciated. The truth is that gifts remain what they are whether they are liked or not. They continue to carry their blessings and abilities. By neglecting a gift, we do not take away its potential for blessings, fulfillment, and contentment. We just choose to shortchange ourselves.

People tend to overlook the benefits of being single. They simply choose not to see them. They don't want to be single. They think they won't like it, so they don't give it a chance. These people are so certain that it can't be helpful to them that they refuse it. They don't even try to efficiently and effectively make use of it. Basically, it is not because they can't enjoy it or lack the ability to do so. They simply don't want to. They don't bother to dig up its treasures. And most end up rushing into marriage.

People don't like the thought of remaining single. In many cases, they actually think of it as a curse. The Bible says, "Sing, O barren one, who did not bear; beak forth into singing and cry aloud, you who have not been in labor! For the children of the desolate one will be more than the children of her who is married, says the Lord" (Isa. 54:1 ESV).

The word *barren* means "sterile or impotent." The word *one* in the phrase "Sing, O barren one" refers to one as an entity, a single individual, one person. Anything that is "one" is single, be it an object, a character, or a type of situation, for it has its peculiarity. Its peculiarity is in its potency and singular state. Its efficacy lies in its nature. That is why it stands out. It has its own strength and completeness as a brand of its own. Being single is an opportunity to do exploits for the Lord. Such exploits will be marked with our own personality, character, and uniqueness.

Anything done with a "single" purpose either by a group or institution has an effectiveness and potency. Single is a strong word that has nothing to do with incompleteness. A single entity is not incomplete. It simply means it has *strength* of its own. (See Colossians 2:9-10.)

A purpose or goal can be *singular.* It is a sole item. Anything done with *singleness of mind* is normally *distinct,* whether done by a group of people or a person. Look at any nation that has a singular purpose or goal. Unity is formed and progress is the result. Why? Because of the word *single*. It is a strong word.

Let us look at the nation of Israel. Though it consisted of twelve tribes, it had a "singular purpose." That was to leave Egypt. They *all* put the blood of the lamb over their doors, and the Bible records that *none* of them died when the death angel passed over their houses and wiped out *all* the first born of the Egyptians. All the Israelites left Egypt together. (See Exodus 12.) After Egypt, the Israelites continued to act with a singular purpose. They marched— one and all—around the walls of Jericho without saying a word. When they had gone around seven times, they all let out a great shout and the walls of Jericho fell down! (See Joshua 6.)

During the reign of Queen Esther, *all* the Jews fasted for three days to overturn the king's written decree for their destruction. (See Esther 4:16.) These masses of people had a *singular* purpose. They had a singular goal and were of a singular mind. Every time they acted with a singular purpose, it was effective! It *never* failed. When there was a diversion or a division, the results were not good. "Single" is a bond. A single goal and a single mind are difficult to break, for they are complete on their own.

A single thing can be said to be *separate*. Separate does not mean incomplete, remember. It means something is sufficient in itself. It can survive on its own. Let us look at "two individuals." The word "individual" signifies one. Now let's look at "two individuals," both complete and sufficient in themselves. They are *separate*, each functioning independently of the other. I pray that God opens our eyes that we may see the beauty that is ours as *one whole individual entity*. We are whole. We are full as a person. We are God's own. To be single is beautiful because it represents a full, complete personality. A person.

Let's use clubs as an example. Some clubs admit members based entirely on certain criteria. These clubs are *exclusive* for members *only*. These members met *specific criteria*, which defines the group as a whole. Members of this club have one agenda and one club name. Though they are many, they act as one, making that club separate and uniquely different from other clubs. It stands out for a *peculiar* reason or *criteria*. It is single in purpose, whole and complete in the midst of other clubs.

There are many facets of the word *single*. Its meaning is like a polygon. It is like a person. *Single* has character, zest, and determination. Anywhere it goes, *zest* and *determination* follow. This is a sure way of detecting it. It always makes itself distinct. It is content to fulfill its singular goal.

Being single or alone does not mean you should refuse help from others. To be single does not mean to be *single-handed*. You can depend on people along the way. There is a saying that no man is an island unto himself. Interacting is natural. It does not sway goals. Paul accepted help; in fact he needed help, but his mind was so dominating and singular in his resolve to win the Gentiles that nothing could stop him from preaching. No circumstance, no human being, and no fear could sway him. Everything *became* a tool for him. Even his trials helped to mature him.

To be single should not be a burden. You can ask for and receive help when you need it. Jesus was single. He had disciples. We, as singles, interact freely with others, having no restraint in our hearts or attitudes that would convince us to remain unattached. We are free to love all people and show it. Nothing can hinder us from our goal. We are limitless. We can choose to be.

Understanding the meaning of being single is like opening your eyes to a new wide world full of mysteries that only you who desire or crave to remain unattached can appreciate. Only by your need, willingness, and understanding can you enjoy it. It is not the curse it is thought to be. It should never be despised in youth or old age. It should be enjoyed. Accept it as a friend rather than an enemy. You have to understand a friend to be able to walk happily together whether for a short or long while!

You should know, too, that married or not, you will definitely need this brand of strength. This is a God-given ability. That is why you have to tap from it now. In solitude, in your soberness, in identification, throughout your life, you will fall back to it. Married or not, when you have need of a personal decision or opinion, you will depend on your inner self in the Lord to pull you through.

Everyone at one time or another makes personal decisions about situations and relationships. You will one day stand before the judgment seat of Christ, as will we all. At that time, you will account for yourself and yourself alone, your thoughts, words, and deeds. In a way, *you are always single.* Learn that. It is an innate ability in everyone. You will always have that part in you, even when you are with the one you marry. To be single is that *uniqueness* only you have. It is your flair. Discover it and conquer the world. Melody Green was single for ten years after the death of her husband Keith. She conquered!

Unmarried Men and Women

Let's take a look at some unmarried people, those who through their gifts and abilities did great exploits for the Lord. Matthew 19:11-12 says:

> *He said to them, "All cannot accept this saying, but only those to whom it has been given: for there are eunuchs who were born thus from their mother's womb, and there are eunuchs who were made eunuchs by men, and there are eunuchs who have made themselves eunuchs for the kingdom of heaven's sake. He who is able to accept it, let him accept it"* (NKJV).

Kathryn Kuhlman was one of the greatest. She was married for a time, but her marriage didn't work out. She was extremely close to the Holy Spirit. They were one! To her, the Holy Spirit was more real than you or anyone who could be *seen*. Above everything else, let us seek to learn this *oneness*. Let's have our own *individual* closeness and worship time with the Lord—one so personal, so unique that it cannot be learned from any man or church (but infinitely ours). Kuhlman lived as a single most of her life. She was better known as a single woman than a married one. Great miracles, healings, revivals, and revelations took place during her meetings. When she walked in front of people, many would fall under the anointing. Virtue and power oozed out of her. Her very being was involved—her heart, strength, emotions, and mind.

Ellen G. White was another great woman of God from the 1700s. She wrote the books *The Desire of Ages* and *The Great Controversy*. You ought to read these books to see the powerful revelations recorded there. Few men or women have received revelations like these. She was definitely a woman who lived close to God's heart.

Chung Syn, which means "bright promise," is a Chinese woman who vowed to God to be single. She does not regret it. She wrote her biography, which relates the great challenges she experienced throughout her life. She is a living witness to God's faithfulness, even more so since she is blind! You must read her book.

Dr. Helen Roseveare is a Christian missionary who pioneered vital medical work in the rainforests of the Democratic Republic of Congo, formerly known as Zaire. Her zeal ruled her. Her life illustrates that singleness is both a gift and an ability. Very few could do what she did, and even fewer would try. She was driven by the gift that was inherent in her. Dr. Roseveare wrote *Living Sacrifice*, *Living Holiness*, and *Give Me This Mountain*. These books ought to be read. Her life is a testimony.

There are many women and men out there with *this capacity*. Most are not encouraged. They are afraid to step out into the deep. They don't share their heart's desires or conflicts because of the fear they might be thought of as abnormal. Choosing not to marry is more or less a taboo, the dreamer's world! There are many out there who have lived and who are even now living out their lives as singles. Many are serving as missionaries in faraway places. There are many who have made this choice and have given themselves to the Lord's work, living and dying in obscurity. Only the Lord knows their stories. He will reward them on that great day. These courageous saints should be appreciated and applauded.

It does not matter whether you are known or not; what matters is what you are doing and the measure of your heart toward God.

Gabrielle Tinkle, who wrote *Delivered to Declare*, is another living example. All these people lived happy lives. They have a song to sing and a testimony to give—one worthy of emulation. They cannot be despised in our eyes because they are unmarried. It would be a shame to do so.

Anna, the daughter of Phanuel, a prophetess, is a biblical example of someone who excelled as a single. (See Luke 2:36-38.) She was of a great age, having lived with her husband seven years from her virginity *and as a widow* until she was eighty-four. She did not depart from the temple, worshipping with fasting and prayer night and day. She and Simeon, the priest, a devout and righteous man, were among the few who recognized the baby Jesus as the long-awaited Messiah. Because of her closeness to the Lord, she was able to perceive that the baby Jesus was the promised Messiah.

Jephthah's daughter is another biblical example. (See Judges 11:29-40.) She gave in to her father's vow to the Lord just like Isaac allowed his father Abraham to tie him up to be sacrificed. She bewailed her virginity in the mountains and then gave herself to fulfill his vow. What a child! God honors such people.

Why did they allow this? Why did they allow their father? Because it was God to whom the supreme sacrifice was to be given. Psalm 50:5 says, "Bring My faithful people to Me—those who made a covenant with Me by giving sacrifices" (NLT). None of the people mentioned above lived a *vain* life. Quite the opposite, they *inspire* us. Their lives are proof that if the married live good purposeful lives, how much more those who are single! We all have that ability. (See First Corinthians 7:7.)

Let us look at the unmarried males. The apostle Paul wrote most of the books in the New Testament and conquered half the world for Christ. He turned it right side up! Paul says, "I wish that all men were even as I myself" (1 Cor. 7:7 NKJV). The reason is seen in verses 32-33: "I want you to be without care. He who is unmarried cares for the things of the Lord—how he may please the Lord. But he who is married cares about the things of the world—how he may please his wife" (NKJV). The primary answer lies in verse 35, though, which says, "This I say for your own profit, not that I may put a leash on you, but for what is proper, and that you may serve the Lord without distraction" (NKJV).

Whether single or married, you can serve God better without distractions. Some are distracted because they are single. Others are distracted because they are married. Those who cannot remain single do not sin if they marry. It is a blessing, just as remaining single is a blessing. The Bible says that both are good. Neither is a curse! Know who you are and seek a balanced life. That's all God asks of you.

Paul, in his defense, states, "Do we have no right to take along a believing wife, as do also the other apostles, the brothers of the Lord, and Cephas?" (1 Cor. 9:5 NKJV). This can only mean one thing: Paul and Barnabas were unmarried, and it wasn't a curse. They chose to forfeit this right for the sake of the Gospel. (See First Corinthians 9:5-12.)

Yet Paul had *hidden* knowledge of the married. He advised both the unmarried and married. All knowledge comes from Christ, thank God! He gives abundantly to those who ask Him. Deuteronomy 29:29 states, "The secret things belong to the Lord our God, but *those things which are revealed belong to us and to our children* forever, that we may *do all the words of this law*" (NKJV).

Paul also has a great deal of advice for those who are married! How can this come from a man who never married? It is possible! The secret things belong to God. We can know all things. That is why we should not despise anything that comes from God. (See Psalm 25:14; Jeremiah 33:3, First Corinthians 2:12,15-16.) He gives us the insight and wisdom we need. We are the most balanced of all people because we are God's people. Paul wrote:

> *Husbands, love your wives, just as Christ also loved the church and gave Himself for her…. He who loves his wife loves himself. For no one ever hated his own flesh, but nourishes and cherishes it, just as Lord does the church. For we are members of His body, of His flesh and of His bones. For this reason a man shall leave his father and mother and be joined to his wife, and the two shall become one flesh* (Ephesians 5:25,28-32 NKJV).

This is a profound mystery that can *only come* from a man of *depth* and knowledge. He knew all things and conquered almost half the world for Christ through the Holy Ghost. He was single, yet he was balanced. He had depth because of the Holy Spirit that lived richly in him because *he allowed* Him great access. I recommend that you read the Book of Acts if, as a single man or woman, you want to see what can be done by one single person. Read it through without paying attention to chapters. This is a sure way to learn about the exploits and adventures of the apostle Paul. Read the other letters and epistles Paul wrote as well.

Paul and Barnabas are shining examples of what dedicated single men can do. They worked side by side with Peter and the rest. Because of Paul, we who are Gentiles have had a chance to hear the Gospel. He started out boldly, launched into the deep, and the Gospel reached down to us! He was a man after the heart of God. Let's launch into the deep whatever it may be!

Let us look at David Brainerd, missionary to the American Indians. He inspired great men like Charles Finney, the prayer warrior. David was an inspiration, though he lived only 29 years.

How many more unattached single Christians died while doing the work of the Lord? We have no way of knowing, but likely the number is great. Many died who were known only to God. And there are plenty more today who are full of the Spirit and producing much fruit. "You will know them by their fruits" (Matt. 7:16-20 NKJV). These were men *whose lives had power,* unlike those talked about in Second Timothy 3:5, which says: "Having a *form of godliness* but denying its *power"* (NKJV). They are not like those described in Colossians 2:18: "Taking delight in false humility and worship of angels, intruding into those things which he has not seen, vainly puffed up by his fleshly mind" (NKJV).

So long as you *love* God with all your *heart, mind, and strength,* no matter your *denomination,* you do not belong on the list above. So long as you have made the *decision* to sacrifice and separate yourself by the purity of your heart for God's work, you are following Him and have a sweet relationship with Him (without deceit). You are acknowledged by Him!

In this particular calling, evidences should be seen in your life, not deceit. Instead of living in deceit, it is better to marry, for it is no sin. God understands. Your time to leave the single status is up. Your single phase is finished, and you have blazed your trail. Don't be tossed about by what other people think.

Let us look briefly into some Scriptures that support the single status as a life mission for the Gospel. These will not only support you but comfort you as well.

For the eunuch: "But He [Jesus] said to them, 'Not all men can receive this saying, *but only those to whom it has been given*'" (Matt. 19:11 NKJV). Jesus Himself said here that not all men can receive this saying but only those to whom it has been given— meaning those who were given the gift of singleness. Jesus went further and said:

> *There are eunuchs who have been so from birth, and there are eunuchs who have been made eunuchs by men, and there are eunuchs who made themselves eunuchs for the sake of the kingdom of heaven. Let the one who is able to receive this receive it* (Matthew 19:12 ESV).

The Scripture above shows that there are three types of eunuchs described by Jesus:

- Those who are eunuchs from birth.

- Those who are made eunuchs by men.

- Those who make themselves eunuchs for the Kingdom of Heaven.

The Scripture in Matthew 19 also says that there are those who are able to receive this gift. Jesus infers here that eunuchs don't marry and choose not to or are not able to produce children. However, Jesus ended this statement by saying that it is only for those who are able to receive it. This means if you are able to receive it, you are also capable *of living* it. It is possible for a human being, but not all human beings.

In this chapter, Jesus was answering the disciples' question concerning the married. Jesus told them that married couples were no longer two but one and that what God had joined together *no human being* should separate. Read Matthew 19:4-12. This is a must! Marriages *were* meant to be forever. Note that in verse 8, Jesus said that Moses gave permission to divorce because their hearts were hardened toward each other, but *it was not like that at the time of creation.*

God takes the mating and joining of a husband and his wife very seriously. Let us learn to be like God and forgive all things. Our hearts can be big enough. Ask yourself how many times you have deserted God and followed other things: men, friends, women, career, money, possessions, to name a few. It is like adultery to God if you have an intimate relationship with Him and then leave Him. You should not put other things before Him. He should come first. God forgives us. Let us learn to do the same with the ones we love.

We do not follow society. We belong to God.

A Call to Single Adults

A call to singles should be this: *stay in love* with the Lord. Don't just love Him. In-love emotion signifies intensity, remember? If you are asked if you have seen the Lord, your answer should be yes! For you speak with Him and live with Him. Yes, indeed you have seen the Lord. This passionate, intense relationship should always be worked on. When you are in love with Him, your heart longs for His presence. Indeed, some of those who are passionately in love recognize even the footsteps of those they love.

There is a difference between being in love and just loving someone. He who is in love is more *sensitive* to hurts and happiness. Our *in love* should not consist only of the human physical concept. We should be in love with God, too. Everything started with Him. God was *in love* with man and made him for fellowship—a willing fellowship that should be out of *choice* from our hearts. God is still *in love* with man.

"What is man [oh Lord] that You are mindful of him?" (Ps. 8:4 NKJV). *Love* made God create man, and *love* made Jesus die on the cross for us. The *symptoms* of being *in love* are not necessarily all caught up in *eros*. They are also the beautiful emotions that come from God's agape love. Sin is what soiled things. These symptoms of *eros* are God-injected, God-known, and God-felt.

God is love utterly! Before you call, He hears. Some would say that is *telepathy*. He *searches* our hearts because of love. He is mindful of us. (See Psalm 8:4.) He will do so much *more* than you ask of Him. If you asked for bread, He would not give you a scorpion. Love is what makes Him *give* and *give* and *give.* Can you see and understand yet? His heartbeat is *for* you! God bares Himself to you with all His sensitivity, so much that you can hurt Him. (See Ephesians 4:30.) He gives both to the good and bad, caring little how much you return once you get to *know* Him, love Him willingly, and obey Him. Obedience is *bound* to love. They go hand in hand. God made His love unconditional. This is what God is. This is His nature.

Remember the great secret, that being in love made God create Eve for Adam. God wanted the best for him. He first made the beasts, the animals, yet there was none found as a helper *fit* for him. In Genesis 2, the sequence of creation is seen. Genesis 2:18 says, "Then the Lord God said, It is not good that the man should be alone; I will make him a helper fit for him" (ESV). "Out of the ground the Lord God formed every beast of the field and every bird of the air, and brought them to Adam to see what he would call them" (Genesis 2:19 NKJV). Have you ever wondered why Eve and the animals were made? It was for the companionship of Adam!

We have to thank Adam's *loneliness* for some creations! However, God is all-knowing, and by His *counsel* all things are and were made. God saw that none of the animals were a suitable helper for Adam. Then we read:

> *The Lord God caused a deep sleep to fall upon the man, and while he slept took one of his ribs and closed up its place with flesh. And the rib that the Lord God had taken from the man he made into a woman and brought her to the man. Then the man said, "This at last is bone of my bones and flesh of my*

flesh; she shall be called Woman because she was taken out of Man" (Gen. 2:21-23 ESV).

The animals were made out of the ground but Eve was *more.* She is the only creation made *out of the being* of another living creature even as both were created after God's image and likeness, male and female.

It was being *in love* that made God perform this heart and body surgery. The animals were *not* a fit for Adam. God Himself said so. Though animals are friends to man and some scientists would say they bear a resemblance, they were not like Adam. This is because God created the animals for company, with the intention of keeping Adam interested, inquisitive, and busy. God decided to give Adam his heart's request. God's own banquet gift—from His heart to Adam—was Eve. He made this gift so good and perfect that He had to take Adam's rib and cause him to "sleep." God certainly took time and consideration before making Eve.

Eve is beloved of God, from God's very heart. A lover gives and gives to overflowing. God was in love, so He gave and still gives to overflowing. He didn't stop with Eve. He gave Himself, Jesus, and the Holy Spirit to meet your needs, your wants, and your desires. That is a part of being in love. I believe that to be in love is the greatest thing on earth. It is right and beautiful. How I wish you could see this love through God's eyes, standing in His place so that you can feel what He feels for you.

I believe that *eros* love comes from the *agape* love of God, His unconditional love. God cannot accept lukewarm love from His loved ones. He wants the first fruits of your love. He wants to be loved above all things. He paid the price for the sin that caused the separation. He has done all He can do. Anything He does not do is left for us—you and me!

I cannot overemphasize this type of love God has for us mortal beings. It's an all-consuming love that makes Him a jealous God.

This love is what God demands of us. After all, we are made in His image. We are His type! (See Deuteronomy 6:5.) This is especially important for the single person whose heart is free. As a single individual, you should be constantly *in love* with our God. You will achieve a great deal this way. It is the only way you can appreciate fully the gift of being single. I believe in your ability to love your singleness. I believe singleness is a gift. If it were not, it would not be in the Bible.

I think fear, uncertainty, fragility, and yes, the pressures of living make people, both great and small, keep their lips sealed on this issue. They are afraid of being wrong or leading people astray. It is of course a hard road to take. It should not be taken as a do-or-die thing. It is best when a person goes on as he or she is and lets things work themselves out. Keep listening to the Lord and occupying the territory He has given you. Decisions should be left for the inner man, to be made with His guidance. Meanwhile, don't deceive yourself. Let the Lord be your source of strength in the road you choose: single, separated, widowed, or married.

Specific Promises for Singles Who Are Eunuchs

*Let not the eunuch say, "Behold, I am a dry tree." For thus says the Lord: "To the eunuchs who keep My Sabbaths, who choose the things that please Me and hold fast My covenant, I will give in My house and **within My walls a monument and a name better than sons and daughters**. I will give them an **everlasting name that shall not be cut off**"* (Isaiah 56:3-5 ESV).

What a wonderful promise! A promise that is engraved cannot be wiped out or removed. People turn blind eyes to this promise, but not you. You, precious one, have made your decision and know your pathway—that of a eunuch! Indeed, this promise is *wholeheartedly yours*! Within His walls and house, you will have a monument and a name better than sons and daughters. What more can you ask? The promise speaks for itself. Imagine having a name better than what you could have possibly desired, an everlasting name that shall *not be cut off.*

This promise is for those who have chosen to be *eunuchs*—eunuchs who keep the Sabbath, choose the things that please God, and hold fast to His covenant. Did you know that there was a covenant between God and eunuchs? It is a covenant that every child of God has *plus* their own *personal* covenant! That is why God says next, "I will give in My house and within My walls a monument and *a name better than sons and daughters*" (Isa. 56:5 ESV). Paul, in his letter to the Corinthians on questions regarding marriage, says this:

> *If any man thinks he is behaving improperly toward his virgin, if she is past the flower of youth, and thus it must be, let him do what he wishes. He does not sin; let them marry. Nevertheless he who stands steadfast in his heart, having no necessity, but has power over his own will, and has so determined in his heart that he will keep his virgin, does well. So then he who gives her in marriage does well, but he who does not give her in marriage does better* (1 Corinthians 7:36-38 NKJV).

Paul in the beginning says he speaks as one who has the Spirit of God but not as a commandment. (See First Corinthians 7:6,25.) Four things are seen running through these verses regarding the married and unmarried:

1. The person who desires to marry should have a strong passion for the other person. It is not God's intention for people to marry who wish simply to live like brothers and sisters. In addition to the *agape* type of love, God wants you to also have a blend of erotic passion or *eros* love. The Bible says, "If his *passions are strong*; and *it has to be,* let him do as he wished: let them marry—it is no sin" (see verse 36).

2. For those who marry, it is not a sin. In fact, they are told that they are doing a good thing! Paul says it would help

them refrain from temptation; to marry is to do well (see verse 38). For the person who desires to remain single, the Bible says he does better (see verse 38)! "And he who refrains from marriage will do even better" (ESV). This means that there is a possibility that the unmarried person can produce better and perform better than the married, even though Paul himself said it was good to be married.

3. Only he who is firmly established in his heart, being under no necessity but having his desire under control, has the right and ability to refrain from marriage. Only *those* can do better. However, it is no light matter merely for exuberant Christians. Age and maturity will press hard, and God doesn't want to see you fail. This is why this decision should be made by a mature Christian rather than a new believer. God wants us to know the cost. Jesus said that it was only the foolish man who builds a house without first counting the cost. Eventually the builder will not be able to finish his house. Know the cost so that you can budget well and be able to finish your building.

4. Those who decide to be eunuchs for the Gospel's sake *do have* desires. It does not mean he or she is physically impotent! He was not after all *born impotent*, neither was he made a eunuch (impotent) by men. (He is not physically castrated.) Eunuchs who make themselves eunuchs for the Kingdom *choose* this with all their normal and physical reactions intact. When such emotions and passions arise, they don't think they are abnormal or curse themselves! Praise God, they are normal. It's the body saying, "Hey, I am around, you know!" But, *a eunuch* is firmly *established* both in heart and head! And that person is under no necessity, pressure, or doubt of his course, and his desires are under *control*.

I am repeating and emphasizing the criteria here, not only for those who make themselves eunuchs but also for all eunuchs, those born, those made, and those who by choice made themselves eunuchs! This ability is a gift, a God-given gift not many can receive or decide to receive. They shy away because they already know they are not able. Likewise, eunuchs should know *beyond reasonable doubt* that they are eunuchs and *can* make it from deep within their hearts. They *should not* be afraid. Eunuchs are *human beings*; they are *not* abnormal. They are *very close* to God's heart. They have *clear* promises from God. (See Isaiah 56:3-5.)

Let us look at another promise. This one is fantastic because it contains joy. God demands that they rejoice! Be filled with joy and gladness!

> *"Sing, O barren one, who did not bear; break forth into singing and cry aloud, you who have not been in labor! For the children of the desolate will be more than the children of her who is married," says the Lord* (Isaiah 54:1 ESV).

This passage says "break forth into singing," and it can only mean one thing. If you are a eunuch, you should rejoice with all your being, with all you've got! Those who are to do this are those who have not been in travail. Travail means they have not tasted the travail of childbirth. They have *never* been pregnant, not that they were and had a miscarriage! Barren is not being able to produce or have seed. This is what the Lord says, "Your children shall be more than of the *married*." This means He is talking to the *unmarried*! Not those who have seed. However, *both* are covered by this verse.

Praise God for eunuchs: their children shall definitely be more than those of the married. Blessed are the seeds of their labor— labor for souls and the labor of their hands. They have large hearts to accommodate others and their children, having had none of their own. They have beautiful feet to spread the Gospel.

(See Isaiah 52:7.) Their lives are songs. If you choose this direction, you can be sure you were made for it. *Be not discouraged!*

I wish all men's eyes would open to the "nature of the hope" to which they have been called. There is wealth if only we know. To whichever state we are, He is the one who has called us. Black, white, no matter the race, married or single, rich or poor, short or tall. Let us look into the Bible once more.

Ephesians 1:18-20 (NIV) says: "I pray also that the eyes of your heart may be enlightened in order that you may know the hope to which He has called you, the riches of His glorious inheritance in the saints." *(May you know, may your eyes be opened that you may comprehend—this is a revelation and an understanding of Him!)* Continuing on: "That you may know…His incomparably great power for us who believe. That power is like the working of His mighty strength, which He exerted in Christ when He raise Him from the dead and seated Him at His right hand in the heavenly realms."

This is a powerful reality because of the truth that we are raised together with Him in heavenly places far above all names, powers, and authority in this world and the next. (See Ephesians 2:6.) I recommend that you read the Book of Ephesians. It is an eye-opener for all Christians, both single and married.

Let us look at another lovely passage in the Bible, which says that loving God pays off and working for Him pays off in this life. First Timothy 4:8 says: "For bodily exercise profiteth little; but *godliness is profitable unto all things*, having promise of the life that now is, and of that which is to come." The Bible tells us that bodily exercise in any form is profitable. It in no way condemns bodily exercise. It does help to keep your "house" fit for yourself and for the Kingdom. But look what the Bible says about *godliness*. It is the purity of the heart. Any godly exercise is *profitable whatever it costs* you. The Bible says it is profitable for this life *and* for the life to come. Godliness is an *eternal value.*

I believe strongly that the Lord will perfect that which concerns you. Psalm 138:8 says: "The Lord will perfect that which concerneth me: Thy mercy, O Lord, endureth for ever; forsake not the works of thine own hands." There is no need to worry or strain your soul. "All things work together for good to them that love God, and them who are the called according to His purpose" (Romans 8:28).

Learn in whatever situation or circumstances you find yourself to keep your mind in perfect peace. God is always working in you! It is He who is at work in you if the fruit of the Spirit abounds in your soul. (See Galatians 5:22.) His grace is definitely sufficient for you. In His grace you stand. In His grace you will survive. Second Corinthians 12:9 says, "My grace is sufficient for thee, for My strength is made perfect in weakness."

Another encouraging verse is in Second Corinthians 4:7: "We have this treasure in earthen vessels, that the excellence of the power may be of God and not of us" (NKJV). You are the earthen vessels. Your strength comes from the Lord. John rightly says, "Without me [Christ] ye can do *nothing*" (John 15:5). Therefore, rejoice because all His abilities are yours. He takes the glory. Your boasting is of Him.

Let us now look at some Old Testament Scriptures. Numbers 18:6 says, "And I, behold, I have taken your brethren the Levites from among the children of Israel: to you they are given as a gift for the Lord, to do the service of the tabernacle of the congregation." These people are like those of you who know you are eunuchs. Eunuchs are gifts to God and from God. They are equally gifts to mankind. "To the congregation" means to the children of God, the brethren. They are gifts from God to uplift and stir our spirits. They are blessings. Eunuchs are gifts, not only from God, but back to God. They are to be examples, to be emulated. Their character and dedication are a light to the brethren and a sweet aroma to God.

Proverbs 17:8 states that "a gift is as a precious stone in the eyes of him that hath it: whithersoever it turneth, it prospereth." What more happiness can you have? Wherever this gift leads you, you will prosper! Another supporting verse can be seen in Proverbs 18:16, which says, "A man's gift makes room for him, and brings him before great men" (NKJV).

As a gift, it will bring you good things and great opportunities. It will open doors for you and make room for you and *bring* you before great people. Conquer them for God!

No matter who you are or what your resource, God will open the way before you where there is no way so that you have opportunity to advance the Kingdom as He has called you. You have something to give! If it isn't of God, it will crumble. (See Acts 5:38-39.) But if it is truly from God, it will endure forever. Nothing can be added to it or taken from it. Let your case rest here as you move along with your zeal and love for God. Let nothing stop you. Whatever God does endures forever! Please remember these other important passages in the Bible:

> *I have loved you with an everlasting love; I have drawn you with loving-kindness* (Jeremiah 31:3 NIV).

> *Since you are precious and honored in My sight and because I love you, I will give men in exchange for you, and people in exchange for your life* (Isaiah 43:4 NIV).

> *I am convinced that neither death nor life, neither angels nor demons, neither the present nor the future, nor any powers, neither height nor depth, nor anything else in all creation, will be able to separate us from the love of God that is in Christ Jesus our Lord* (Romans 8:38-39 NIV).

If you have sinned and your conscience condemns you, remember that Jesus intercedes for you. (See Hebrews 7:25; Romans 8:34; First Timothy 2:5.) You can come *boldly* to the throne of grace and receive *mercy* in time of need. (See Hebrews 4:16.)

In First John 3:19-20, we read: "This then is how we know that we belong to the truth, and how we set our hearts at rest in His presence whenever our hearts condemn us. For God is *greater than our hearts,* and He knows everything" (NIV).

God is faithful and just to forgive us all our sins, but like First John 2:1 says, "I write this to you so that you will not sin" (NIV). Remember, we have the capacity to live the life God wants us to as single, unattached Christians. Check out this verse from Second Peter 1:3: "His divine power has given us everything we need for life and godliness through our knowledge of Him who called us by His own glory and goodness" (NIV).

"Through our knowledge of Him" who called us by His own glory and goodness, He has indeed given us singles *everything* we need for life and godliness. Let's thank God for that.

Every unattached Christian should have this as their *motto*: "Let us cast aside the sin which so easily besets us and lift up the hands which hang down and the feeble knees and make straight paths our ways." (See Hebrews 12:12-13.)

Let us say, "I have come in the volume of the book that is written of us to do Thy will, O God!" God said this rightly of you:

> *Before I formed thee in the belly I knew thee; and before thou camest forth out of the womb I sanctified thee.... See, I have this day set thee over the nations and over the kingdoms, to root out, pull down, and to destroy, and to throw down, to build, and to plant* (Jeremiah 1:5,10).

You have been wonderfully and beautifully made. Hallelujah! Folks, let us fill our streets with every facet of God's dream! (See Psalm 139:14.)

FINAL NOTE

As you mature, you probably will become surer of your desires and views in life. But most likely you will also become more responsible and knowledgeable. That's what really counts. What does not count is your independence *away* from the Lord. This begins as a rather slow but subtle change. It can be identified by these telltale signs:

- You no longer view things in terms of God and satan. You become so independent in your thinking that you cease to believe satan can tamper with your life. You depend too much on your own decisions and abilities (state of mind). You feel too much has been blamed on evil spirits or demons (wrongly or rightly so).

- You no longer see the need for fellowship or attend Christian gatherings.

- You are no longer affected by the gentle correction of your brethren.

- You are bored or irritated by most preaching. You have become hard of hearing.

- You feel everything is normal, and you go on with your activities.

- You feel a strong sense of boredom.

If you recognize any of these signs in your life, you are at risk of falling prey to this subtle "independence." Note that a less mature Christian is not at the risk of this isolation! You have to know where to strike the balance. There is a throne in your life, and someone is on it—is it you, God, or satan?

My final note to every man and woman who reads this book is that you ought to be *responsible*. This is the key word for the mature individual. Don't be distracted by a fear that you will become fixed and independent (set in your ways) or so used to your own company and decisions that you would not be able to tolerate another person or view in your life. As you grow, your character solidifies. Your needs and view of life become rather *fixed*. But that doesn't mean you will be unsuitable for marriage in your later years. Dismiss the idea that you wouldn't be able to find someone close to your ideal. No matter how *grown up* or *mature* you become or *what situation* you find yourself in, stay close to the Lord and continue your intimacy with Him. Whether you marry or not, you will be just fine.

CONTACT THE AUTHOR

E—mail address:
azukapassions@yahoo.com

A new exciting title from
DESTINY IMAGE™ EUROPE

WALKING ON WITH JESUS
90-Day Devotional Journey From God's Heart to Your Heart

by *Rosalie Willis Storment*

God created you for loving fellowship and longs to speak to your heart. There is nothing more exciting in life than walking with God, sitting in His Presence daily and asking, "Father, what is on Your heart for me today? What is it You want me to know?" Or, "Dear Father, how do I respond to this difficult situation?" He is always with you to comfort, encourage, and give you wisdom and understanding.

Walking on With Jesus represents many years of writing down every precious word received, and daily walking in loving, intimate relationship with Him. Each word He speaks is a treasure never to be forgotten, but to be enjoyed, learned from, and read over and over again. His Words impart comfort, direction, wisdom, correction, strength, character, love, delight, grace, faith, hope, patience, healing, and life, causing you to become a transparent reflection of His love, peace, and joy. Through it all, He teaches you how to love His treasures—His people—as He does, with truth, faithfulness, forgiveness, and honor.

ISBN: 978-88-89127-92-6

A new exciting title from
DESTINY IMAGE™ EUROPE

BEYOND LIMITS
Discover Life's Winning Strategies
by *Lami Abayilo*

There is a higher place for you to live. In this realm you not only see the mountaintop, you see from the mountain top. From this view nothing is impossible and no problem is insurmountable.

God designed this place especially for you. It is a place far above the overwhelming complexities of life. This is a realm beyond limits.

Beyond Limits helps you discover how to:

- Stop life's downward spirals.
- Fulfill your life's visions and dreams.
- Rise to the top, despite all resistance, and so much more.

Living beyond the limits we and others place on us is to live in His presence where there is joy and peace beyond imagination.

ISBN: 978-88-89127-66-7

Order now from Destiny Image Europe
Telephone: +39 085 4716623 - Fax: +39 085 9431270
E-mail: orders@eurodestinyimage.com

Internet: www.eurodestinyimage.com

Additional copies of this book and other book titles from DESTINY IMAGE™ EUROPE are available at your local bookstore.

We are adding new titles every month!

To view our complete catalog online, visit us at:
www.eurodestinyimage.com

Send a request for a catalog to:

Via Acquacorrente, 6
65123 - Pescara - ITALY
Tel. +39 085 4716623 - Fax +39 085 9431270

"Changing the world, one book at a time."

Are you an author?

Do you have a today, God-given message?

CONTACT US

We will be happy to review your manuscript for the possibility of publication:

publisher@eurodestinyimage.com
http://www.eurodestinyimage.com/pages/AuthorsAppForm.htm